Favorite Family Recipes

A YEAR OF
FAVORITES

Published by Covenant Communications, Inc.
American Fork, Utah

Printed in China
First Printing: September 2018

23 22 21 20 19 18   10 9 8 7 6 5 4 3 2 1

ISBN-13: 978-1-52440-800-8

Favorite Family Recipes

A YEAR OF
FAVORITES

ECHO BLICKENSTAFF, ELISE DONOVAN, EMILY WALKER & ERICA WALKER

INTRODUCTION

Whether it is a quick dinner on a busy night or an elegant meal celebrating a holiday or birthday, food brings a family together. The gathering of a family to enjoy food is where the magic happens. We eat. We talk. We share. We are all in the same place at the same time doing the same thing.

MAKING FOOD | MAKING MEMORIES

We all agree that our most cherished times are when we gather as a family, and those gatherings always include good food. We have sweet memories of our Grandpa and Grandma Edwards, who loved to go on picnics with their family. Because of them, our Edwards family reunions always include gathering in a beautiful place to enjoy a potluck picnic. We are fortunate to have fabulous cooks and bakers in the family, resulting in picnics that abound with good food and good people!

Our Grandpa and Grandma Kidman also knew how to draw in those they loved with good things to eat. Grandpa Kidman loved black licorice and gladly shared with his grandchildren who were willing to try it. Grandma Kidman had a candy dish by her front door. Grandchildren, great-grandchildren, and neighborhood children loved to be greeted at her door with a warm smile and a treat. We miss our grandparents, but we are grateful for the wonderful memories!

Our mother, Linda Kidman Edwards, is the inspiration for all of us. She welcomes family and friends to her dinner table to celebrate birthdays, holidays, and achievements. There is always something special on the menu. Beautifully decorated birthday cakes, homemade spaghetti sauce with her garden-grown tomatoes, chocolate chip cookies on Sunday afternoons, chili and hamburgers on Dad's birthday, locos tacos on camping trips, homemade peanut-butter-filled chocolate eggs at Easter, and clam chowder on Christmas Eve are just a few of the things we look forward to each year. Those traditions keep her children and grandchildren close to her and close to each other. Our dad, Dale Edwards, is always close by to offer his services as a taste-tester or to help cook something on the grill. He is also the number-one, greatly appreciated helper when it is time to clean up!

SERVE AND CELEBRATE THE PEOPLE YOU LOVE

Every season and every month provide reasons to gather family and friends. We created this cookbook to share our favorite family recipes for each month of the year—recipes we prepare for our families when we spend time together. Cooking for others is one of the greatest gifts you can give them. The time invested in shopping, food prep, cooking, and cleanup is significant—but that investment is always worth it! When you make something great, it brings everyone to the table for Sunday dinner, a family breakfast, or a slice of pie on the front porch.

You and your family also have favorite recipes and food traditions. It is our hope that you will use this cookbook to record the treasured recipes that bring your family and friends together. Please make this cookbook unique to you and your family! We have included blank recipe sections at the end of each month for you to add your favorite family recipes. Each month these pages can remind you to you to make food that will make memories for your family!

ELISE DONOVAN, EMILY WALKER,
ECHO BLICKENSTAFF & ERICA WALKER

TABLE OF CONTENTS

CHAPTER 1

JANUARY

January

THE FIRST MONTH OF THE YEAR,

A perfect time to start all over again,

CHANGING ENERGIES AND

DESERTING OLD MOODS,

New beginnings, new attitudes.

—Charmaine J. Forde

In January, we celebrate the beginning of a new year. Our family has a tradition of eating Chinese food on New Year's Eve or New Year's Day. We're not sure how the tradition started, but for some reason, Chinese food tastes really good after all the classic ham and turkey meals we eat during the holidays.

January is a time for a fresh start. For most of us, our resolutions for the new year tend to be focused on taking better care of ourselves physically. Eating healthier doesn't mean we have to give up delicious food. Quite the contrary! We've included some of our favorite recipes this month that are nutritious and satisfying. Because Australia Day is in January, we've added our recipe for Australian Sausage Rolls. Emily's husband, Beau, lived in Australia for a couple of years and brought this recipe back with him.

SLOW-COOKER
CASHEW CHICKEN

SERVES
4

¼ C. all-purpose flour

½ tsp. black pepper

2 lbs. chicken breasts, cut into bite-size pieces

1 T. canola oil

¼ C. soy sauce

2 T. rice vinegar

2 T. ketchup

1 T. brown sugar

1 garlic clove, minced

½ tsp. fresh ginger, grated

¼ tsp. red pepper flakes

½ C. cashews, unsalted

Combine flour and pepper in a resealable plastic bag. Add chicken. Shake the bag to coat the chicken with the flour mixture. Heat oil in a skillet over medium-high heat. Brown chicken about 2 minutes on each side. Place chicken in a slow-cooker. In a small bowl, combine soy sauce, vinegar, ketchup, brown sugar, garlic, ginger, and red pepper flakes; pour mixture over the chicken. Cook on low for 3–4 hours. Stir in cashews just before serving.

SHARE YOUR FAVORITE JANUARY RECIPES WITH YOUR FAMILY AT THE END OF THE SECTION.

What are your favorite recipes for celebrating the new year?

PANDA EXPRESS
CHOW MEIN
Copycat Recipe

¼ C. soy sauce

1 T. brown sugar

2 cloves garlic, minced

1 tsp. fresh ginger, grated

Ground black pepper to taste

3 5.6-ounce pkgs. refrigerated Yaki Soba noodles

2–3 T. vegetable oil

⅔ C. celery, chopped diagonally

1 medium-size onion, thinly sliced

2 C. chopped cabbage

In a small bowl, combine soy sauce, brown sugar, garlic, ginger, and black pepper. Set aside.

Remove Yaki Soba from packages and discard flavoring packets. Rinse noodles well, drain, and set aside. Heat oil in a large wok or skillet. Add celery and onion and sauté for 1–2 minutes, or until onions start to become soft and transparent. Add cabbage and sauté an additional minute or so. Toss Yaki Soba noodles and soy sauce mixture with the vegetables over medium-high heat for an additional 2–3 minutes, or until noodles are heated through.

GOLDEN
DETOX SMOOTHIE

SERVES
1

1 banana

2 T. honey Greek yogurt

1 carrot, peeled and diced

½ C. fresh pineapple

½ C. fresh-squeezed orange juice

½ C. water

Ice cubes, optional

Thoroughly mix all ingredients in a blender. Pour into a glass and enjoy!

SHARE YOUR FAVORITE JANUARY RECIPES WITH YOUR FAMILY AT THE END OF THE SECTION.

*What are your go-to recipes
when you want to eat healthier?*

LIGHT FREEZER BREAKFAST
SANDWICHES

2 16-oz. tubes Turkey Breakfast Sausage

9 eggs

9 egg whites

1 C. milk

Salt and pepper to taste

24-pack Fiber One English Muffins

24 cheese slices (we use Kraft 2% Milk American Cheese Slices)

Sliced tomato (optional)

Preheat oven to 375 degrees. Press the turkey sausage evenly into the bottom of a 13 x 18 baking sheet; the sausage should completely cover the bottom of the pan. Bake for about 15 minutes. The sausage should be browned and should pull from the sides of the pan. While the sausage is baking, beat the eggs, egg whites, milk, salt, and pepper in a bowl. Spray another 13 x 18 baking sheet with nonstick cooking spray. Pour the egg mixture into the pan. Carefully place the eggs in the oven and bake for 15 minutes, or until the eggs are no longer runny. Cut the sausage and eggs into 24 equal squares. Open each English muffin and add a slice of sausage, egg, and cheese to each one. Put each sandwich into a resealable sandwich-size plastic bag. When all of the sandwiches are prepared and stored in bags, freeze the sandwiches in a large resealable plastic bag, airtight plastic container, or cardboard box to help prevent freezer burn.

When ready to eat, remove from freezer and plastic bag. Wrap in a paper towel and microwave for 1 minute 30 seconds on defrost (30 percent power). Turn over and microwave on high for another 60–90 seconds. The sandwiches can also be defrosted overnight in the refrigerator; wrap the defrosted sandwich in a paper towel and microwave on high for 90 seconds.

Optional: add a fresh tomato slice to the sandwich before serving.

GREEK YOGURT DIP

Copycat Recipe

SERVES
16

½ red bell pepper

½ green bell pepper

1 onion

3 jalapeño peppers (remove seeds for a mild flavor)

1 bulb garlic (7–8 cloves)

¼ C. olive oil

1 15-oz. can roasted tomatoes, drained well

1 T. paprika

2 T. canola oil

Salt to taste

48 oz. plain Greek yogurt

Preheat oven to 400 degrees. Slice bell peppers, onion, and jalapeño peppers; place on a baking sheet. Cut off the top of the garlic bulb and place cut side up on the baking sheet with the vegetables. Drizzle olive oil over all the vegetables and garlic. Bake for 25–30 minutes. Scoop out roasted garlic from the bulb (it will be hot) and place with the other roasted vegetables in a blender or food processor. Add roasted tomatoes, paprika, canola oil, and salt to the blender; blend until smooth. Slowly fold the mixture into the plain Greek yogurt. Add more salt if needed. For best results, refrigerate in an airtight container overnight.

WEIGHT LOSS
MAGIC SOUP

1 small onion

2 cloves garlic, minced

8 oz. mushrooms, sliced

3 carrots, peeled and sliced

32 oz. chicken broth (use low-sodium if desired)

3 C. V-8 juice

28 oz. Italian diced tomatoes

1 zucchini, diced

1 yellow squash, diced

2 C. green beans, fresh or frozen

1 14-oz. can kidney beans, drained and rinsed

3–4 C. shredded cabbage

1 tsp. Italian seasoning

Salt and pepper to taste

In a large frying pan sprayed with cooking spray, sauté onions, garlic, mushrooms, and carrot for about 5 minutes. In a large slow-cooker, combine sautéed garlic and vegetables with the remaining ingredients. Cook on high for 2–3 hours, or until vegetables are fork-tender.

This makes a large batch of soup. If you would like to freeze portions of it to use later, undercook the vegetables just a little. Pour the soup into resealable freezer bags and let as much air out as you can. Lay the bags flat on a cookie sheet and freeze. Once the soup is frozen, it is easy to layer in your freezer. To thaw, place the bag in the refrigerator for 24 hours and reheat.

ONE-POT CREAMY
GARLIC NOODLES

SERVES
6

4 T. butter, divided

4–5 cloves garlic, minced

28 oz. chicken broth

2 ½ C. milk, more if needed

1 lb. linguine noodles

Kosher salt and black pepper
to taste

1 tsp. basil

⅔ C. Parmesan cheese

4 C. broccoli, optional

2 chicken breasts, grilled and
cut into strips, optional

In a large 5–6-quart skillet or stock pot, heat 2 T. butter over medium heat. Add garlic and cook for about a minute. Add chicken broth, milk, remaining 2 T. butter, noodles, salt, pepper, and basil. Bring to a boil, stirring occasionally. Once boiling, reduce heat to a simmer; cook, stirring occasionally, for 16–20 minutes, or until noodles have cooked through.

Stir in Parmesan cheese when noodles are finished cooking. Add a little milk if necessary to reach desired consistency.

If you want to add broccoli and/or chicken, stir it in 10 minutes into the simmering process.

SPAGHETTI SQUASH
LASAGNA

3 spaghetti squash, medium-size

Salt and fresh pepper to taste

⅓ C. part-skim ricotta cheese

2 T. grated Parmesan cheese

1 T. chopped parsley or basil

Sauce:

1 tsp. olive oil

½ onion, finely chopped

3 cloves garlic, minced

14 oz. Italian chicken sausage, reduced-fat sausage, or lean ground beef

1 14-oz. can crushed tomatoes

Salt and fresh pepper to taste

2 T. fresh chopped basil

3/4 C. mozzarella cheese, shredded

Preheat oven to 400 degrees. Cut spaghetti squash in half lengthwise and scoop out seeds and fibers. Season cut side lightly with salt and black pepper. Bake for 1 hour, cut side down. If you prefer to cook the squash in the microwave, cut squash in half lengthwise, scoop out seeds and fibers, and place on a microwave-safe dish. Cover and microwave 8–9 minutes, or until soft. In a small bowl, combine ricotta cheese, Parmesan cheese, and parsley or basil.

To make the sauce, in a large, deep sauté pan, heat oil and add onions and garlic. Sauté on medium low for 3–4 minutes or until onions are clear and soft. Add the sausage and cook, breaking up into smaller pieces, until brown. Add crushed tomatoes, salt, and pepper to taste. Reduce heat to low and simmer 20–30 minutes. Add fresh basil.

When spaghetti squash is cooked, let it cool for about 10 minutes, keeping the oven on. If you microwaved the squash, preheat the oven to 400 degrees. When the spaghetti squash is cool enough to handle, use a fork to remove flesh, which will come out in strands that look like spaghetti. Set the squash shells aside. Drain the squash on a paper towel to soak up any excess liquid, then toss with half of the sauce in a large bowl. Scoop the spaghetti squash and sauce mixture back into the shells. Place the shells on a baking sheet. Top with remaining sauce, 1 scoop ricotta cheese mixture, and a little mozzarella cheese. Bake 30–35 minutes.

GUILT-FREE
OATMEAL COOKIES

ABOUT
4
COOKIES

3 ripe bananas, mashed

⅓ C. applesauce

2 C. oats

3 T. milk

1 tsp. vanilla

1 tsp. cinnamon

½ C. raisins or chocolate chips

Preheat oven to 350 degrees. In a large mixing bowl, combine all ingredients. Stir until well combined and the consistency of cookie dough. Place spoonfuls of mixture onto a greased cookie sheet. Bake 15–20 minutes.

AUSTRALIAN
SAUSAGE ROLLS

1 pkg. frozen puff pastry
1 ½ lbs. pork sausage
¾ C. Italian bread crumbs
⅓ C. milk
1 tsp. garlic, minced
½ tsp. paprika
Salt and pepper to taste

For the egg wash:
1 egg
1 T. water
Paprika

Preheat oven to 425 degrees. Follow the directions on the puff pastry package to thaw dough correctly. Unfold dough onto a lightly floured surface. There should be 2 big squares. Cut each square in half, making 4 long rectangles. In a large bowl or food processor, combine sausage, bread crumbs, milk, garlic, paprika, salt, and pepper. Mix until all the ingredients are thoroughly incorporated. Divide the sausage mixture evenly into 4 sections. Place a long tube of sausage mixture in the middle of each pastry rectangle. Roll the pastry up over the sausage and pinch the seam together, creating 4 long logs. Cut each log into 4 equal sections or rolls. Place the rolls on a cookie sheet lined with parchment paper.

To make the egg wash, mix the egg and water together. Brush each roll with the egg wash. Sprinkle a little paprika on each roll. Bake at 425 for 5 minutes, then reduce heat to 350 degrees and bake for 30–35 minutes longer. Drain some of the grease from the sausage halfway through the baking time. Rolls should look puffed and golden. The sausage in the center should be fully cooked. Remove rolls from pan and place on paper towels to cool.

In Australia, these are traditionally eaten plain or dipped in ketchup. They are also delicious dipped in marinara sauce, Alfredo sauce, country gravy, or cheese sauce.

SHARE YOUR FAVORITE JANUARY RECIPES WITH
YOUR FAMILY AT THE END OF THE SECTION.

*Have you visited other countries
and brought back recipes to enjoy?*

FAVORITE FAMILY RECIPE

SERVES

_____

{ RECIPE TITLE }

Ingredients:

_____
_____
_____
_____
_____
_____
_____
_____
_____
_____
_____
_____
_____
_____
_____
_____
_____
_____

Instructions:

_____
_____
_____
_____
_____
_____
_____
_____
_____
_____
_____
_____
_____
_____
_____
_____
_____
_____
_____
_____
_____

FAVORITE FAMILY RECIPE

SERVES

{ RECIPE TITLE }

Ingredients:

_____

_____

_____

_____

_____

_____

_____

_____

_____

_____

_____

_____

_____

_____

_____

_____

_____

_____

Instructions:

_____

_____

_____

_____

_____

_____

_____

_____

_____

_____

_____

_____

_____

_____

_____

_____

_____

_____

_____

CHAPTER 2

FEBRUARY

February

WITHOUT VALENTINE'S DAY,

February would be . . .

WELL, JANUARY

—Jim Gaffigan

Julia Child once said, "I think careful cooking is love, don't you? The loveliest thing you can cook for someone who's close to you is about as nice a Valentine as you can give." We heartily agree. A candlelight dinner with Spinach Artichoke Cheese Fondue, Filet Mignon, and one of our chocolate cakes for dessert would cause anyone to fall head over heels in love! Other favorite recipes for Valentine's Day include our Chicken Parmesan Stuffed Shells and our version of Nothing Bundt Cakes' White Chocolate Raspberry Cake. So many lovely recipes make it so hard to choose when there's only one Valentine's Day a year!

February also brings the Super Bowl, a fun time to gather and cheer on your favorite team—and no Super Bowl party is complete without food. Try our Loaded Cheesy Potato Skins or Sweet and Spicy Appetizer Meatballs to snack on during the game.

LOADED CHEESY
POTATO SKINS

SERVES
4

4 medium-size potatoes

1 cube butter, melted

1 C. cheddar cheese, shredded

1 C. bacon, cooked and crumbled

Sour cream, optional

Chives, optional

Preheat oven to 425 degrees; bake potatoes for 1 hour. When cool, cut the potatoes in half and scoop out the center, leaving about a ¼-inch layer of potato in the shell. Brush the entire potato with melted butter and put under the broiler for 6–8 minutes until lightly browned. Sprinkle cheese and bacon on each potato half. Broil for 1–2 minutes longer or until cheese is melted. Serve with sour cream and chives if desired.

SHARE YOUR FAVORITE FEBRUARY RECIPES WITH YOUR FAMILY AT THE END OF THE SECTION.

Does your family have a favorite game day appetizer?

SERVES
8

SWEET AND SPICY APPETIZER
MEATBALLS

25–26 oz. precooked frozen meatballs

⅓ C. Frank's Original Hot Sauce (no substitutions)

1 ½ C. packed brown sugar

1 T. water

Place meatballs in slow-cooker. In a medium bowl, combine hot sauce, brown sugar, and water; stir until well combined and sugar is mostly dissolved. Pour evenly over meatballs. Cover and cook on low 4–5 hours or on high 2–3 hours.

THE MELTING POT'S
SPINACH ARTICHOKE
CHEESE FONDUE
Copycat Recipe

SERVES
8

1 ½ C. vegetable broth

1 C. loosely packed fresh spinach, chopped

¾ C. artichoke hearts, chopped

1 tsp. minced garlic

7 oz. Butterkäse cheese, grated (may substitute farmer's cheese or Romanian cream cheese, or see substitution below)

1 5-oz. pkg. Parmesan cheese blend, grated (be sure first 2 ingredients listed are Parmesan and fontina cheese)

In fondue pot or similar cooking pot, heat vegetable broth but do not bring to a boil. When hot, add spinach, artichoke hearts, and garlic; mix well. Continue to cook until the spinach and artichokes hearts soften. In a large bowl, combine the grated cheeses; add to the broth a little bit at a time, stirring constantly. Continue melting and stirring until you have added all the cheese and the consistency is smooth and creamy.

Serve with French bread pieces, steamed vegetables, cooked meat, chips, pretzels, or crackers.

Substitution for Butterkäse Cheese: mix ½ brick (4 oz.) cream cheese with ¼ C. buttermilk and ½ T. sour cream.

FANCY
FILET MIGNON

SERVES
2

2 cuts filet mignon, 1 to 1 ½ inch thick

Dry rub, to taste (see recipe below)

1 C. balsamic vinegar

¼ C. brown sugar

1 C. mushrooms, sliced

1 C. onions, sliced

3 T. butter

Sliced green onion or chives for garnish

Creamy Blue Cheese Sauce (see recipe below)

Dry Rub

½ tsp. paprika

½ tsp. ground mustard

½ tsp. sugar

½ tsp. brown sugar

¼ tsp. cumin

¼ tsp. cayenne

½ tsp. pepper

Creamy Blue Cheese Sauce

⅓ C. mayonnaise

⅔ C. sour cream

1 ½ tsp. Worcestershire sauce

4 oz. blue cheese, crumbled

Let the filets rest out of the refrigerator for 30–40 minutes prior to grilling. When the filets are brought to room temperature, rub the dry rub generously onto each piece. Grill over medium heat to desired doneness. Do not overcook; the filets will taste best with a pink center. If preferred, you can sear the filets and bake in the oven at 300–350 degrees until they reach the desired doneness. Check often. Remove from heat and allow filets to sit about 3 minutes to let the juices settle into the filet.

In a medium saucepan, mix balsamic vinegar and brown sugar. Bring to a slight boil over medium heat, stirring constantly until sugar is dissolved. Reduce heat to low and simmer for 15–20 minutes until reduced to a syrupy consistency and half the original volume. While the glaze is simmering, sauté mushrooms and onions in butter until onions become soft and transparent. Remove from heat.

Layer Creamy Blue Cheese Sauce and sautéed onions and mushrooms over filets. Drizzle with balsamic reduction. Top with green onion.

Optional: Serve with mashed potatoes and/or cooked asparagus.

DRY RUB: In a small bowl, mix all ingredients.

CREAMY BLUE CHEESE SAUCE: In a saucepan over low heat, combine mayonnaise, sour cream, and Worcestershire sauce. Stir until smooth and warmed. Remove from heat and stir in the blue cheese crumbles. Spoon over filet mignon or serve on the side for dipping.

CARNIVAL CRUISE LINE CHOCOLATE

MELTING CAKE
Copycat Recipe

SERVES
4

¾ C. dark chocolate chips

¾ C. butter

4 eggs, room temperature

¾ C. sugar

⅛ tsp. vanilla extract

¼ C. flour

Preheat oven to 375 degrees. In a small saucepan, melt chocolate chips and butter; cool 10 minutes. In a separate bowl, whisk eggs, sugar, and vanilla. Add flour and whisk until completely mixed in. Stir cooled chocolate mixture into egg mixture.

Divide cake batter into 4 7-oz. ramekins, filling each ramekin about ¾ full. Bake for 14 minutes. Cake should be spongy on top but gooey in the middle. Do not overcook. Serve with ice cream.

SHARE YOUR FAVORITE FEBRUARY RECIPES WITH YOUR FAMILY AT THE END OF THE SECTION.

Do you have a favorite chocolate cake recipe?

FLOURLESS
CHOCOLATE CAKE

8 eggs
1 C. butter
16 oz. Ghirardelli semisweet chocolate chips
1–2 tsp. almond extract
¼ C. heavy cream
1 C. Ghirardelli semisweet chocolate chips
Powdered sugar
Fresh raspberries

Preheat oven to 325 degrees. Beat eggs for several minutes on high until thick, fluffy, and a light-yellow color. Set aside. In a microwave-safe bowl, melt butter; immediately add the 16 oz. semisweet chocolate chips. Stir until chocolate is smooth and completely melted. If necessary, microwave in 15-second increments to finish melting the chocolate. While still mixing, slowly add the chocolate to the whipped eggs until completely combined. Use a rubber spatula to scrape the sides. Stir in almond extract.

Prepare an 8-inch round cake pan by thoroughly buttering the bottom and sides. Cut out a round piece of parchment paper for the bottom and a long strip to line the inner side of the pan; butter those also. Pour the batter into the cake pan. Bake at 325 degrees for 30–35 minutes, or until it doesn't feel like there is any liquid underneath when you lightly touch the center.

While the cake is baking, prepare the ganache topping: In a glass bowl, microwave the cream for 1 minute, or until it just begins to boil at the edge of the bowl. Remove from microwave and immediately add 1 C. chocolate chips. Stir until the chocolate chips are completely melted.

Remove cake from oven and let it stand at room temperature for at least 30 minutes before spreading the ganache topping evenly over the top of the cake, leaving a small rim around the outer crust. Chill in the refrigerator for at least 3 hours. Sprinkle cake with powdered sugar and top with fresh raspberries before serving.

MINI CHERRY
CHEESECAKES

SERVES
18
CAKES

18 vanilla wafers

2 eggs

2 tsp. vanilla

1 C. sugar

16 oz. cream cheese, softened

Cherry pie filling

Place 18 cupcake liners in muffin tins. Place a vanilla wafer, flat side down, in the bottom of each liner. In a medium bowl, beat eggs, vanilla, sugar, and cream cheese until smooth. Fill each liner ⅔ full with the cheesecake batter. Bake at 350 degrees for 15 minutes. Remove from oven and cool. Top each mini cheesecake with cherry pie filling. Keep refrigerated until ready to serve.

SHARE YOUR FAVORITE FEBRUARY RECIPES WITH YOUR FAMILY AT THE END OF THE SECTION.

What is your favorite Valentine's Day dessert or treat?

NOTHING BUNDT CAKE'S
WHITE CHOCOLATE
RASPBERRY CAKE
Copycat Recipe

1 box white cake mix
1 5-oz. pkg. instant white chocolate pudding mix
1 C. sour cream
4 large eggs
½ C. water
½ C. oil
1 ½ C. white chocolate chips chopped into smaller pieces
1 C. raspberry pastry filling
2 8-oz. pkgs. cream cheese, softened
½ C. butter, softened
2 tsp. vanilla
3–4 C. powdered sugar
Fresh raspberries

Preheat oven to 350 degrees. In a mixer or bowl, combine first 6 ingredients. Fold in white chocolate chips. Pour half of the batter into a well-greased bundt cake pan (nonstick cooking spray works great). Spoon half of the raspberry filling in small, separate spoonfuls over the batter. Using a knife, swirl the filling through the batter. Pour remaining batter evenly over the top and spoon in remaining pie filling, repeating the swirling process.

Bake 45–50 minutes, or until toothpick inserted in the center comes out clean. If toothpick doesn't come out clean, bake an additional 3–5 minutes until it does. Allow cake to cool for 20 minutes. Remove cake from bundt pan by placing a plate upside down over the bundt pan. While holding the plate firmly on top of the bundt pan, flip both over so the cake comes out onto the plate. Cover the cake with plastic wrap and place it in the refrigerator overnight before frosting.

In a medium bowl, cream the cream cheese and butter until creamy. Mix in the vanilla. Gradually stir in the powdered sugar, starting with 2 C. and gradually adding more until the frosting is nice and thick. Spoon the frosting into a gallon-size resealable plastic bag. Clip one bottom corner of the bag. Squeeze frosting out of the bag onto the cake in large strips, starting on the edge of the cake and ending in the middle so each cake piece that will be cut will have a thick frosting layer. Fill the hole in the center of the cake with remaining frosting. Top with fresh raspberries.

PEANUT BUTTER
BONBONS

SERVES
8

2 C. graham cracker crumbs

4 C. powdered sugar

1 C. flaked coconut

1 C. butter, softened

1 tsp. vanilla

1 C. creamy peanut butter

White, dark, or milk
chocolate, if desired

In a large bowl, mix graham cracker crumbs, powdered sugar, and coconut. Add butter, vanilla, and peanut butter; stir until completely combined. Roll or press mixture into 1-inch balls. Refrigerate to set or serve immediately. If desired, dip in melted white, dark, or milk chocolate.

BEEF NOODLE
STIR-FRY

Sauce/marinade:
⅔ C. reduced-sodium soy sauce
⅔ C. beef broth
2 T. brown sugar
4 cloves garlic, minced
2 tsp. ginger, minced
1 tsp. cornstarch

Stir-fry:
1 lb. linguine noodles
1 lb. boneless beef sirloin steak, sliced thin
4 tsp. canola oil, divided
1 red bell pepper, sliced thin
1 onion, sliced thin
2 carrots, sliced into matchsticks
2 C. broccoli florets
1–2 C. cabbage, shredded
Sesame seeds to taste, optional

To make marinade: In a small mixing bowl, combine soy sauce, broth, brown sugar, garlic, and ginger. Place half of the mixture in a gallon-size resealable plastic bag. Add sliced steak and seal, pressing out as much air as possible. Refrigerate for at least 2 hours. Add cornstarch to remaining mixture in bowl and stir until smooth. Cover and refrigerate until ready to use.

Prepare linguine noodles according to package directions. While noodles are cooking, heat 2 tsp. oil in a large skillet over medium-high heat and add steak slices. Discard excess marinade from plastic bag. Stir-fry steak until just browned. Remove steak from skillet and set aside. Add remaining oil to the same skillet and stir-fry peppers, onion, carrots, and broccoli until onions become clear and soft. Add cabbage and beef to the skillet and cook until cabbage becomes soft. When noodles are soft, drain and toss with beef/vegetable mixture, adding the reserved sauce mixture. Toss until noodles are coated in sauce. Top with sesame seeds and serve immediately.

CHICKEN PARMESAN
STUFFED SHELLS

SERVES
6

1 16-oz. box large/jumbo pasta shells
8–10 breaded chicken strips, cooked
1 lb. mozzarella cheese in a block
1 quart-size jar spaghetti sauce
Shredded mozzarella/ Parmesan blend, to taste
Fresh basil chopped, to taste

Preheat oven to 375 degrees. Cook pasta shells according to package directions. Drain and allow to cool for easier handling. Cut chicken strips into 1½-inch pieces. Cut mozzarella cheese into strips to desired thickness. Place a strip of cheese on top of each chicken piece and each inside a shell. If needed, use a toothpick to hold the shell and chicken together. Spread about ½ C. spaghetti sauce over the bottom of a 9 x 13 glass baking dish. Place the prepared stuffed shells in the baking dish and cover evenly with remaining spaghetti sauce. Top with shredded cheese blend. Bake for 20–25 minutes, or until sauce is hot and bubbly. Let stand for 5–10 minutes before serving. Top with fresh basil.

FAVORITE FAMILY RECIPE

SERVES

―

{ RECIPE TITLE }

Ingredients:

Instructions:

FAVORITE FAMILY RECIPE

SERVES

_____

{ RECIPE TITLE }

Ingredients:

_____
_____
_____
_____
_____
_____
_____
_____
_____
_____
_____
_____
_____
_____
_____
_____
_____
_____
_____

Instructions:

_____
_____
_____
_____
_____
_____
_____
_____
_____
_____
_____
_____
_____
_____
_____
_____
_____
_____
_____
_____
_____
_____
_____

CHAPTER 3

MARCH

March

BLESS US WITH GOOD FOOD,

the gift of gab, and hearty laughter.

MAY THE LOVE AND JOY WE SHARE

be with us ever after. Amen.

—Irish Kitchen Prayer

The month of March brings lots of reasons to try new recipes in the kitchen. We have Irish blood in our family, and St. Patrick's Day is a fun time to celebrate with either Irish food or at least some green food and desserts. Our whole family loves Slow-Cooker Irish Beef Stew and Irish Soda Bread, and we're confident they will be very popular recipes with your family, too. Finish the meal off with a Shamrock Shake, and everyone will feel they have a little luck on their side.

Mardi Gras is also fun to celebrate with delicious food; try our One-Pot Jambalaya Pasta and Shrimp Po' Boys. Don't forget to finish your Mardi Gras celebration off with some New Orleans Mini Beignets.

If you have sports fans in the family, your family may gather to watch the March Madness NCAA basketball tournaments. Try some new appetizers, like Poutine or White Castle Sliders, on game nights.

POUTINE

Oil for frying

5–6 medium potatoes, cut into strips for fries

2 tsp. salt or seasoning salt

2 C. cheese curds

1½ C. gravy (leftover homemade beef gravy is best, but you can also use the recipe below)

Gravy:

4 T. butter

¼ C. flour

2 C. beef broth

1 tsp. onion powder

Salt and pepper to taste

In a deep fryer or large skillet, heat oil to 360 degrees. Fry potatoes in batches for about 5 minutes each or until golden brown and crispy on the outside; don't overcrowd the potatoes while frying. Place on paper towels to drain excess oil. Season lightly with salt and place on a large platter. Sprinkle cheese curds evenly over fries and pour hot gravy over the top. Serve immediately.

Gravy: In a medium-size saucepan, melt butter over medium heat. Whisk in flour to make a roux. Reduce heat and slowly add beef broth, whisking constantly, until desired thickness is reached. Add onion powder, salt, and pepper to taste. Serve hot.

SHARE YOUR FAVORITE MARCH RECIPES WITH YOUR FAMILY AT THE END OF THE SECTION.

Do you have a favorite appetizer recipe?

MUSHROOM SWISS ROAST BEEF
SLIDERS

Pkg. of 12 Hawaiian rolls
8 oz. fresh mushrooms, sliced
¾ lb. roast beef
½ lb. Swiss cheese
⅓ C. butter, melted
3 cloves garlic, minced
1 tsp. Worcestershire sauce
½ tsp. onion powder

Blue Cheese Horseradish Sauce:
⅓ C. crumbled blue cheese
2 T. sour cream
2 T. mayonnaise
2 T. green onion, chopped
2 T. horseradish
Fresh ground pepper to taste

Preheat oven to 350 degrees. Spray the bottom only of a 9 x 13 baking dish with nonstick cooking spray. Remove from package but do not separate them. Slice the rolls horizontally through the middle so you have 2 flat slabs. Place the bottom slab in the baking dish; set the top slab aside. In a medium-size skillet, sauté mushrooms; set aside. Layer roast beef, sautéed mushrooms, and cheese over the bottom layer. Place the top slab over the sliders. In a small bowl, combine butter, garlic, Worcestershire sauce, and onion powder; mix well. Using a pastry brush, brush butter mixture over the top of the sliders. Cover dish with tin foil and bake for 20–25 minutes, or until cheese has melted.

While sliders are baking, combine all ingredients for Blue Cheese Horseradish Sauce in a small saucepan. Cook over low heat, stirring often, just until blue cheese melts. Remove sliders from oven; serve immediately with sauce on the side.

ONE-POT
JAMBALAYA PASTA

SERVES
4

2 T. oil

1 ½ lbs. chicken, diced

1 red bell pepper, diced

1 onion, diced

1 lb. smoked sausage, sliced

4 ½ C. chicken broth

1 ½ C. tomato sauce

1 can Rotel diced tomatoes
with green chiles

1 T. Cajun seasoning (we like
Tony Chachere's)

1 T. garlic powder

1 T. paprika

1 T. onion powder

Salt and pepper to taste

1 lb. linguine or spaghetti
noodles

1 lb. uncooked shrimp,
peeled and deveined
(optional)

Cilantro

In a large stockpot or large, deep skillet, heat oil over medium heat. Add chicken and cook until white (it doesn't need to be cooked completely through). Add remaining ingredients except shrimp and cilantro; bring to a boil, stirring often. Reduce heat and simmer for 20–25 minutes, or until noodles become soft, stirring often. Add more chicken broth if necessary. If using shrimp, add it about 15 minutes into the simmering process. Garnish with cilantro before serving.

SERVES
4

SHRIMP
PO' BOYS
with Creamy Cajun Sauce

Creamy Cajun Sauce:
1 C. mayonnaise (Best Foods or Hellmann's brand)
⅔ C. ketchup
3 T. horseradish sauce
½ T. Creole seasoning (or to taste)
½ tsp. garlic powder
½ tsp. paprika
1 T. lemon juice

Shrimp:
1/4 C. butter
2 cloves garlic, minced
1 lb. medium to large uncooked shrimp, peeled and deveined
Creole seasoning to taste
4 hoagie rolls or bratwurst buns
Shredded cabbage, lettuce, or spinach

In a medium mixing bowl, combine sauce ingredients until smooth; set aside. In a large skillet, heat butter and garlic over medium heat. When butter is hot and melted, add shrimp. Sprinkle creole seasoning over the shrimp. When shrimp is pink all the way through, remove from heat. Split rolls open and divide shrimp evenly among rolls. Top with the Creamy Cajun Sauce and shredded cabbage.

NEW ORLEANS
MINI BEIGNETS

SERVES
6-8

1 pkg. dry active yeast

¾ C. hot tap water

¼ C. sugar

1 egg, beaten

½ tsp. salt

½ C. evaporated milk

3 ½ C. flour

⅛ C. shortening

Vegetable oil for frying

1 lunch-size paper bag

Powdered sugar for coating

In a small bowl, combine yeast, water, and sugar; let sit until frothy, about 5 minutes. In a large bowl, combine yeast mixture with egg, salt, and evaporated milk. Blend in about half the flour, add the shortening, and mix well. Add the rest of the flour. The dough should be soft but not sticky; add small amounts of flour as needed until dough is no longer sticky. Cover loosely and let the dough rise in the refrigerator at least 3 hours or overnight.

Punch down dough and place on lightly floured surface. Roll into a large square. Using a knife or pizza cutter, cut the dough into 2-inch squares (for full-size beignets, make 4-inch squares). Place squares on a cookie sheet lined with cooking spray and let rise for 30–40 minutes.

In a deep frying pan, heat vegetable oil over medium-high heat. Set out a large plate covered with paper towels and fill a paper bag with about 1 C. powdered sugar. When oil is hot, carefully place several dough squares into the oil; the dough should float to the top and begin to brown within a few seconds. When the edges start to turn a golden brown, quickly flip them over and cook for a few more seconds. Use a slotted spoon to remove dough and place on paper towels. Let drain on paper towels for about 30 seconds, then toss into the paper bag filled with powdered sugar. Fold over the top of the bag and shake to coat; add more powdered sugar as needed as you go. Remove coated pieces to a plate and serve immediately. They taste best served warm!

SERVES
8

IRISH
SODA BREAD

4 C. flour

¼ C. sugar

1 T. baking powder

1 tsp. baking soda

1 tsp. salt

1 T. caraway seed, chopped

⅓ C. butter

1 egg, beaten

⅓ C. sour cream

1 ¼ C. buttermilk

Heat oven to 375 degrees. In a large bowl, mix flour, sugar, baking powder, baking soda, salt, and caraway seed. Using a pastry blender or whisk, cut in butter until thoroughly combined. Mix in the egg, sour cream, and buttermilk until it forms a sticky dough. Remove dough and place on a floured surface. Knead dough until soft, adding more flour as needed. Place dough in a 9-inch round pan or pie dish; cut a deep X in the center. Bake at 375 degrees for about 40 minutes, or until a nice golden brown. Brush with melted butter. Cool at room temperature.

SHARE YOUR FAVORITE MARCH RECIPES WITH YOUR FAMILY AT THE END OF THE SECTION.

What is your favorite
Irish recipe?

SLOW-COOKER
IRISH BEEF STEW

SERVES
4

1 ½ lbs. chuck roast cut into 1 ½ inch pieces, or use pre-cut stew meat

¼ C. flour

2 tsp. salt

1 tsp. pepper

2 T. olive oil

2 lbs. Yukon Gold potatoes halved or quartered, depending on size

1 lb. baby carrots

2 T. butter

1 yellow onion, diced

3 cloves garlic, minced

3 cans beef broth

1 small can tomato paste

2 T. Balsamic or red wine vinegar

1 T. Worcestershire sauce

2 T. cornstarch + 2 T. cold water

1 T. dried thyme

1 tsp. dried parsley flakes

2 bay leaves

Fresh parsley for garnish

Cut roast into 1½-inch bite-size chunks and place in a gallon-size resealable plastic bag. Add flour, salt, and pepper. Shake bag until meat is coated with flour. In a large, heavy-bottom skillet or pot, heat olive oil. Add coated meat and brown each piece on all sides. While meat is browning, cut potatoes and carrots and place both in the bottom of a slow cooker. Layer browned meat on top of the potatoes and carrots. Leave remaining juices in the skillet. Return the skillet to the stove top and add butter; melt butter over medium-high heat. Sauté onions and garlic in the butter. Stir in beef broth, tomato paste, red wine vinegar, and Worcestershire sauce. In a small cup, combine cornstarch and cold water; mix until smooth, then add to the liquid mixture in the skillet to thicken the liquid. Pour all the contents of the skillet over the meat and vegetables in the slow-cooker. Add thyme, parsley flakes, and bay leaves.

Cook on low for 7–8 hours or on high for approximately 4 hours. Check the taste of the broth about 30 minutes before serving. Add salt, pepper, or seasonings as needed. Allow to cook for another 30 minutes after adding seasonings. Remove bay leaves. Garnish with fresh parsley.

CORNED BEEF
SANDWICHES

4 slices rye or black
pumpernickel bread
6–8 thin slices of corned
beef
2 slices Swiss or Havarti
cheese
Coleslaw
Sliced pickles
Homemade Russian Dressing
(see recipe below)

Homemade Russian
Dressing:
1 C. mayonnaise
½ C. chili sauce
2 T. red wine vinegar
1 T. sugar
½ tsp. garlic powder
½ tsp. paprika
2 shakes of Worcestershire
sauce
Black pepper to taste
3 T. chopped dill pickles

Layer corned beef topped with cheese on 2 slices of bread. Place under the broiler in the oven just until cheese starts to melt. Remove from oven and top with coleslaw and sliced pickles. Drizzle with Russian dressing and top with other 2 slices of bread to make 2 sandwiches.

Homemade Russian Dressing: In a blender, combine all ingredients except chopped pickles; blend until smooth. Pour into a medium-size bowl and stir in chopped pickles. Refrigerate at least 3 hours before serving.

KEY LIME
PIE

For the crust:
⅓ C. butter
¼ C. sugar
1 ¼ C. crushed graham crackers

For the filling:
4 large egg yolks
1 14-oz. can sweetened condensed milk
1 lime
¼ C. key lime juice
2 tsp. lime zest
Whipped topping to garnish

For the crust: Melt butter; stir in sugar and add crushed graham crackers. Spread evenly into a 9-inch pie dish, pressing crust onto bottom and sides. Chill for an hour until firm, then bake at 375 degrees for 5 minutes. Allow to cool before filling.

For the filling: Preheat oven to 350 degrees. With an electric mixer, beat egg yolks until they are thick and turn light yellow. Mixing on a low speed, slowly add sweetened condensed milk. Zest 1 lime, then juice it. Pour fresh lime juice into a ½-cup measuring cup, then fill the cup with key lime juice to make a full ½ C. of juice. Gradually add the lime juice and zest to the egg mixture and continue to mix on low speed until blended. Pour the mixture into the prepared pie shell and bake 15 minutes. Remove and let cool. Serve with a garnish of whipped topping and a small slice of lime.

MCDONALD'S
SHAMROCK SHAKE
Copycat Recipe

2 ½ C. low-fat vanilla ice cream

½ C. fat-free milk

¼ C. sugar

¼ tsp. peppermint extract

¼ tsp. green food coloring

Optional toppings: whipped cream, sprinkles, chocolate mint, maraschino cherry

In a blender, mix all but topping ingredients until smooth. Pour into glasses and top with whipped cream and sprinkles, a chocolate mint, or maraschino cherry.

SHARE YOUR FAVORITE MARCH RECIPES WITH YOUR FAMILY AT THE END OF THE SECTION.

Is there a green food you like to make in March?

FAVORITE FAMILY RECIPE

SERVES

_____
{ RECIPE TITLE }

Ingredients:

_____
_____
_____
_____
_____
_____
_____
_____
_____
_____
_____
_____
_____
_____
_____
_____
_____
_____

Instructions:

_____
_____
_____
_____
_____
_____
_____
_____
_____
_____
_____
_____
_____
_____
_____
_____
_____
_____
_____
_____
_____
_____

FAVORITE FAMILY RECIPE

SERVES

{ RECIPE TITLE }

Ingredients:

Instructions:

CHAPTER 4

APRIL

April

THERE ARE FEW

things so pleasant

AS A PICNIC EATEN

in perfect comfort.

—W. Somerset Maugham

With April come the wonderful signs of spring: warm sunshine, blossoms on the trees, and green grass. It's the time and season to enjoy being outdoors again. Grab a blanket and fill a picnic basket or cooler with Egg Salad Sandwiches and head to the park for an Easter egg hunt!

Celebrating Easter is another reason to gather family and friends to enjoy food. Our Slow-Cooker Maple Spiral Ham and Cheesy Potato Casserole make an Easter dinner easy to prepare. For dessert, it is hard to choose between a Classic Carrot Cake, Coconut Cream Pie, or Four-Layer Banana Pudding. As we mentioned in the introduction, one of the things we look forward to at Easter is the Peanut Butter Easter Eggs Mom makes for us. She even personalizes them with our names and decorates them with our favorite colored flowers. Easter provides such beautiful and delicious traditions!

GLUTEN-FREE BLACKBERRY
PANCAKES
with Coconut Yogurt Syrup

SERVES
6

For the pancakes:
1 ¼ C. gluten-free flour
½ C. sugar
½ tsp. salt
1 tsp. baking powder
1 tsp. baking soda
1 ½ C. milk
1 egg
½ C. fresh blackberries,
slightly chopped

For the syrup:
1 ½ C. sugar
1 6-oz. container coconut
Greek yogurt
½ C. butter
½ tsp. coconut extract

Additional toppings:
Fresh blackberries
Coconut flakes

For the pancakes: In a medium bowl, mix all dry ingredients. Stir in milk and egg. Gently stir in blackberries. Heat a griddle or skillet to medium low and spray with nonstick cooking spray. Pour ½ C. batter on griddle for each pancake. Cook until golden brown, then flip to finish cooking.

For the syrup: In a small saucepan, combine sugar, yogurt, and butter; cook over low heat. When sugar has dissolved, turn heat up to medium high and bring to a boil. Remove from heat and stir in coconut extract.

Top pancakes with the Coconut Yogurt Syrup, fresh blackberries, and coconut flakes.

PANI POPO SAMOAN
COCONUT ROLLS

20 frozen dinner rolls
1 10-oz. can coconut milk
1 C. sugar

Coat a 9x13 glass baking dish with nonstick cooking spray and arrange rolls evenly to thaw. Cover with plastic wrap sprayed with cooking spray. Allow to rise until doubled in size; this can take 4–5 hours. If you need the rolls to thaw more quickly, follow the quick-rise instructions on the package of frozen rolls.

Preheat oven to 350 degrees. In a medium bowl, combine coconut milk and sugar; whisk until sugar is dissolved. Pour about 2/3 of the coconut mixture over the rolls and bake for 20–30 minutes, or until golden brown and dough is baked through. Remove from oven and pour remaining coconut mixture evenly over the top of the rolls. The rolls should be sticky and gooey on the bottom. Rolls can be served upside down or right side up.

CHEESY POTATO
CASSEROLE

2 lbs. frozen hash-brown cubes, country style

2 C. cheddar cheese, shredded

3 tsp. salt

Pepper to taste

½ C. butter, melted

1 can cream of chicken soup

1 pint sour cream

½ C. milk

2 C. corn flakes, crushed

1 T. butter, melted

In a large bowl, combine hash browns, cheese, salt, and pepper. In a separate bowl, whisk butter, soup, sour cream, and milk. Stir into hash-brown mixture; pour into a 9 x 13 baking dish. In a medium bowl, combine crushed corn flakes and 1 T. melted butter; sprinkle over potatoes. Bake at 350 degrees for 1 hour.

EGG SALAD
SANDWICH

4 eggs, boiled and peeled

¼ C. mayonnaise

1 T. dill pickles, diced

½ tsp. fresh dill weed, chopped

1 tsp. mustard

Salt to taste

2 large croissants

Butter lettuce

Separate the yolks from the egg whites; chop egg whites into small pieces. Set aside. In a medium bowl, combine egg yolks, mayonnaise, diced pickles, dill weed, mustard, and salt. Beat until smooth. Gently stir the chopped egg whites into the mix. Cut croissants in half. Spoon half the egg mixture into each croissant. Top with butter lettuce leaves and serve.

SHARE YOUR FAVORITE APRIL RECIPES WITH YOUR FAMILY AT THE END OF THE SECTION.

Do you have a recipe for a special salad or sandwich you like to take on picnics?

SLOW-COOKER AU GRATIN
POTATOES
and ham

8 medium potatoes, peeled and sliced

1 onion, chopped

2 C. cooked ham, cubed

1 ½ C. cheddar cheese, shredded

1 can cream of mushroom soup

⅔ C. milk

½ tsp. thyme

Fresh-ground pepper to taste

Spray the inside of a slow-cooker with nonstick cooking spray. Layer half of the potatoes, onion, ham, and cheese. Repeat layers. In a medium bowl, whisk soup, milk, thyme, and pepper. Pour over potato layers.

Cook on high for 3–4 hours or on low for 6–8 hours.

SLOW-COOKER MAPLE
SPIRAL HAM

1 8- to 10-lb. spiral-cut ham
(boneless or bone-in)
1 C. brown sugar
⅔ C. maple syrup
1 C. pineapple juice

Remove ham from packaging and place in a large (7+ quart) slow-cooker. Place ham flat side down in slow-cooker. Generously rub brown sugar all over ham. Pour maple syrup and pineapple juice over ham. Cook for 2–3 hours on low heat. Spoon juices over the ham and cook on low for an additional 30 minutes. Remove from slow-cooker and serve.

SHARE YOUR FAVORITE APRIL RECIPES WITH YOUR FAMILY AT THE END OF THE SECTION.

What is your favorite
Easter dinner dish?

HOT SURFACE

Cooking
Time

Heat
Setting

Desired
Temp

Actual
Temp

PROGRAM

MANUAL

CLASSIC
CARROT CAKE

3 eggs

2 C. flour

2 C. sugar

1 ¼ C. vegetable or coconut oil

2 tsp. baking soda

2 tsp. cinnamon

1 tsp. salt

2 tsp. vanilla

1 C. shredded coconut

1 C. walnuts or pecans, chopped

1 C. crushed pineapple, drained

2 C. raw carrots, shredded

Cream Cheese Frosting:

4 oz. cream cheese, softened

4 T. butter or margarine, softened

1 lb. powdered sugar

1 tsp. vanilla

In a large bowl, beat eggs. Add the next seven ingredients and beat well until smooth. With a mixing spoon, stir in the coconut, nuts, pineapple, and carrots. Pour into a greased 9 x 13 cake pan. Bake at 350 degrees for 50 minutes. While cake is still slightly warm, spread with cream cheese frosting.

Cream Cheese Frosting: Whip cream cheese and butter on medium speed until well combined. Slowly add powdered sugar until the frosting reaches desired consistency. Add vanilla. If the frosting seems too thick, add a little bit of milk until desired consistency is reached.

FOUR-LAYER
BANANA PUDDING

2 bags Pepperidge Farms
Chessman Cookies

6 bananas, sliced

2 C. milk

1 5-oz. box instant vanilla
pudding

1 8-oz. pkg. cream cheese,
softened

1 14-oz. can sweetened
condensed milk

12 oz. whipped topping,
thawed

Line the bottom of a 9 x 13 pan with one layer of Chessman cookies. Place sliced bananas on top of the cookie layer. In a large bowl, combine milk and pudding mix. Stir until smooth. Set aside. In a separate bowl, combine cream cheese and sweetened condensed milk; stir until smooth. Fold in whipped topping. Combine the two mixtures and stir until well ombined. Pour mixture over the banana layer. Top with another layer of Chessman cookies and refrigerate until ready to serve.

COCONUT
CREAM PIE

1 ½ C. half-and-half

1 ½ C. coconut milk (a little
less than 1 can)

2 eggs

3/4 C. sugar

⅓ C. cornstarch

¼ tsp. salt

1 C. flaked coconut, toasted,
divided

1 tsp. coconut extract or
vanilla extract

9-inch prebaked pie shell

Whipped topping:

1 pint whipping cream

⅓ C. powdered sugar

1 tsp. coconut extract

In a medium saucepan, combine half-and-half, coconut milk, eggs, sugar, cornstarch, and salt.

Bring to a boil over low heat (using a double boiler works best), whisking constantly. When it starts to boil a little and thickens to the consistency of a thick pudding (about 15–20 minutes), remove from heat. Stir in ¾ C. toasted coconut and coconut extract. Pour into pie shell and chill for 2–4 hours, or until firm. While pie is cooling, combine topping ingredients and whip with electric beaters. When pie is completely cooled, top with whipped topping and sprinkle with remaining toasted coconut.

SHARE YOUR FAVORITE APRIL RECIPES WITH
YOUR FAMILY AT THE END OF THE SECTION.

*Do you have a favorite coconut
or lemon recipe?*

CHOCOLATE PEANUT BUTTER
EASTER EGGS

1 14-oz. pkg. milk-chocolate-flavored easy-melt wafers
1 C. peanut butter
⅔ C. powdered sugar
⅛ tsp. salt
Royal icing for decorating (optional) (see recipe below)

Royal Icing:
3 egg whites, at room temperature
4 C. powdered sugar
½ tsp. cream of tartar
Food coloring

In a microwave-safe bowl, microwave chocolate wafers for 30 seconds at half power. Stir. Repeat until wafers are completely melted. Spoon melted chocolate into egg molds, coating bottom and sides completely, about ⅛ inch thick. Refrigerate 30 minutes, or until set. Meanwhile, cook peanut butter in microwave-safe bowl for 30 seconds until softened. Stir in powdered sugar and salt until completely blended. When chocolate is set, carefully spoon peanut butter mixture into egg molds and flatten, leaving about ⅛ inch between peanut butter and the top of the egg mold. Spoon additional melted chocolate over peanut butter until covered completely and level with egg mold. Refrigerate another 30 minutes, or until set. Carefully remove from molds. Decorate as desired with royal icing. Do not refrigerate after decorating—refrigeration will cause the icing to become soft and sticky.

Royal Icing: In the bowl of a mixer, combine egg whites, powdered sugar, and cream of tartar. Beat on medium to high speed until the mixture becomes shiny, stiff, and white (7–10 minutes); occasionally stop the mixer and scrape the sides of the bowl. Add food coloring after mixing. Royal icing hardens quickly. To prevent hardening while you are decorating, wet a paper towel or dish towel and use it to cover icing. Depending on the temperature, humidity, and amount of icing used, royal icing will harden within 15–60 minutes after you decorate the eggs.

FAVORITE FAMILY RECIPE

SERVES

{ RECIPE TITLE }

Ingredients:

Instructions:

FAVORITE FAMILY RECIPE

SERVES

{ RECIPE TITLE }

Ingredients:

Instructions:

CHAPTER 5

MAY

May

THE WORLD'S FAVORITE

season is the spring.

ALL THINGS SEEM

possible in May.

—Edwin Way Teale

May is filled with reasons to gather, celebrate, and remember. We celebrate mothers, we celebrate graduates, we celebrate the June brides-to-be. We have just the recipes for these special occasions. Our Blueberry Cream Cheese Coffee Cake is perfect for a Mother's Day brunch. For a bridal shower or graduation party, try our Cheesecake-Stuffed Chocolate-Dipped Strawberries.

In the United States, Cinco de Mayo (May 5) has become a day to celebrate Mexican-American culture with food and music. Our copycat recipe for Cafe Rio Family-Style Burritos will please any crowd; serve them with our Cheater Restaurant-Style Refried Beans and Restaurant-Style Mexican Rice.

On Memorial Day at the end of May, we remember the men and women who died while serving in the armed forces; we also gather to reflect on and honor our loved ones. Because the weather is beautiful this time of year, our families often meet for an outdoor barbecue or picnic after decorating the graves of our loved ones.

CHEATER RESTAURANT-STYLE
REFRIED BEANS

SERVES
4

1 can refried beans

⅓ C. sour cream

1 T. Valentina hot sauce

¾ C. Monterey Jack cheese, grated (or a cheddar/jack blend)

In a saucepan, combine refried beans, sour cream, and hot sauce; heat over medium-low heat, stirring constantly. When the beans are heated through, pour into a glass pie pan or 9 x 9 dish. Top with grated cheese and heat in the oven or microwave until cheese is melted.

SERVES
4

RESTAURANT-STYLE
MEXICAN RICE

3 T. vegetable oil

1 C. long-grain rice, uncooked

1 tsp. minced garlic

½ tsp. kosher salt

½ tsp. cumin

½ C. tomato sauce

14 oz. chicken broth

3 T. fresh cilantro, finely chopped

In a large saucepan, heat oil over medium heat. Add the rice and gently stir until rice begins to lightly brown. Add garlic, salt, and cumin. Continue cooking and stirring the rice until it looks golden. Stir in tomato sauce and chicken broth; turn heat to medium high. Bring the mixture to a boil, then turn the heat to low and cover the pan with a lid. Simmer for 20–25 minutes. Remove from heat and fluff with a fork. Stir in chopped cilantro and serve.

SHARE YOUR FAVORITE MAY RECIPES WITH YOUR FAMILY AT THE END OF THE SECTION.

Do you have a favorite Mexican food recipe?

CAFÉ RIO FAMILY-STYLE
BURRITOS
Copycat Recipe

2 lbs. country-style pork ribs or pork roast
½ C. Coke
1 C. brown sugar
1 C. red enchilada sauce
1 ½ C. rice, uncooked
3 C. chicken broth
Juice of 1 lime
2 cloves garlic
½ bunch cilantro, chopped
2 cans Cuban-style black beans, lightly drained
1 28-oz. can green enchilada sauce
8–10 flour tortillas
2–3 C. Monterey Jack cheese, grated

Sear pork on all sides until browned. In a slow-cooker, combine pork, Coke, brown sugar, and red enchilada sauce. Cook on high for 3–4 hours or on low for 6–8 hours or until pork is tender and shreds easily. Shred pork; place back in slow-cooker and set aside.

In a rice cooker, combine rice, chicken broth, lime juice, garlic, and cilantro; cook until done. (You can also cook the rice on the stovetop following rice package instructions.) Preheat oven to 350 degrees. Evenly spread ¾ C. green enchilada sauce over the bottom of a 9 x 13 glass pan. On each flour tortilla shell, place ¼ C. shredded pork, a scoop of rice, a scoop of black beans, 2–3 T. green enchilada sauce, and a sprinkle of cheese. Roll into burritos. Place burritos in the prepared 9 x 13 pan. Pour remaining green enchilada sauce evenly over the top of the burritos and sprinkle with remaining cheese. Bake 20–25 minutes or until cheese is hot and bubbly. Serve with remaining rice and beans.

WHITE CHOCOLATE RASPBERRY
FRIED ICE CREAM

1 2-quart container of white chocolate raspberry or vanilla ice cream

1 large container of fresh raspberries, rinsed and dried

1 14-oz. box Cinnamon Frosted Flakes (or Frosted Flakes mixed with 1 tsp. cinnamon) crushed into small pieces

1 C. roasted and lightly salted almonds, chopped fine

6 T. butter, melted

White Chocolate Fudge Sauce (see recipe below)

White Chocolate Fudge Sauce:

1 14-oz. can sweetened condensed milk

1 pkg. white chocolate chips

½ C. light corn syrup

1 tsp. vanilla

Place the ice cream in a large bowl at room temperature and stir it occasionally until the ice cream becomes soft, but not melted. Gently stir in half of the raspberries; reserve the other half for later. In another large bowl, stir the crushed cereal, chopped almonds, and melted butter until thoroughly mixed. Pour half of the cereal mixture into the bottom of a 9 x 13 metal or aluminum pan; gently press evenly along the bottom. Spoon the ice cream over the top and carefully spread it evenly. Sprinkle the remaining half of the cereal mixture over the top, spread evenly, and lightly press it over the ice cream. Cover the pan with aluminum foil and freeze for at least 3 hours or overnight before serving. Cut into squares to serve. Drizzle white chocolate fudge sauce over each piece and top with leftover fresh raspberries.

White Chocolate Fudge Sauce: In a large saucepan, combine first three ingredients. Cook over medium heat until chocolate chips melt and sauce thickens. Remove from heat and stir in vanilla. Serve warm.

BLUEBERRY CREAM CHEESE
COFFEE CAKE

SERVES
12

Batter:

1 C. butter

1 C. sugar

2 eggs

¼ C. sour cream

2 tsp. baking powder

½ tsp. salt

2 C. flour

1 small carton fresh
blueberries, rinsed and dried

Filling:

2 8-oz. pkg. cream cheese

1 egg

1 C. sugar

1 tsp. vanilla

Crumb Topping:

¼ C. sugar

½ C. flour

¼ C. butter

Preheat oven to 350 degrees. Coat a 9 x 13 glass pan with nonstick cooking spray.

Batter: Cream butter and sugar; beat in eggs and sour cream. Add baking powder and salt and mix in. Add flour a little at a time until completely mixed in. Gently fold in the fresh blueberries.

Filling: Beat all ingredients until smooth.

Crumb Topping: Mix all ingredients with a pastry blender or fork until crumbly.

To assemble, spread half the batter into the bottom of the 9 x 13 pan. Spread the cream cheese filling over the top. Evenly spoon the remaining batter over the cream cheese filling. Sprinkle the crumb topping over everything. Bake 50–55 minutes. Cool before serving.

SHARE YOUR FAVORITE MAY RECIPES WITH YOUR FAMILY AT THE END OF THE SECTION.

What is your favorite recipe from your mother?

MOM'S
MACARONI SALAD

SERVES
8

1 lb. macaroni or pasta shells

1 ½ C. mayonnaise

2 T. mustard

¼ C. sour cream

2 T. apple cider vinegar

2 T. sugar

½ tsp. kosher salt

Ground black pepper to taste

1 C. ham steak, cut into cubes

1 C. cheddar cheese, cut into cubes

⅔ C. frozen peas, thawed

2–3 carrots, shredded

Optional mix-ins:

Cucumber, peeled and diced

Dill pickles, chopped

Tomato, diced

Red bell pepper, diced

Celery, chopped

Prepare macaroni al denté according to package directions. Drain well and cool to room temperature. In a medium mixing bowl, combine mayonnaise, mustard, sour cream, apple cider vinegar, sugar, salt, and pepper. Set aside. In a large bowl, toss macaroni with ham, cheese, peas, carrots, and any other mix-ins you desire. Fold in mayonnaise mixture until pasta is well coated. Cover with plastic wrap and allow to sit overnight. If the salad seems dry after setting up overnight, add a little milk until salad becomes nice and creamy again.

ALLIGATOR
JAWS

Dough:
1 T. yeast
⅛ C. warm water
¾ C. lukewarm milk
¼ C. sugar
½ tsp. salt
1 egg
3 T. shortening
3 C. flour
Vegetable oil for frying

Glaze:
¼ C. milk
1 tsp. vanilla
2 C. powdered sugar

Cherry Buttercream Frosting:
6 maraschino cherries
(jarred)
2 T. maraschino cherry juice
(jarred)
½ C. butter, softened to
room temperature
1 lb. powdered sugar

Dough: In the bowl of a mixer, dissolve yeast in water. In a separate bowl, combine milk, sugar, salt, egg, and shortening; add to yeast mixture. Slowly add flour; mix on low until dough is smooth and elastic. Cover with a clean dishtowel and let rise in a warm place until doubled, about 1 hour. Roll dough out on a floured surface to about ½ inch thickness. Cut into tall triangles about 2–3 inches wide by 4 inches tall. Place triangles on a cookie sheet; let rise about 30 minutes. Heat vegetable oil to 375 degrees. Prepare glaze while rising. Slowly transfer the triangles with a spatula to the hot oil. Fry 30 seconds on each side or until they light golden brown.

Glaze: In a medium saucepan, combine milk and vanilla; heat over low until warm. Sift powdered sugar into milk mixture. Whisk slowly until well combined. Remove the glaze from the heat. Dip fried triangles into the glaze one at a time and set on a draining rack placed in a half-sheet pan until cooled.

Cherry Buttercream Frosting: In a food processor, process the cherries with the cherry juice (about 5 pulses). Place the processed cherries in a mixing bowl and combine with butter and about 1 C. powdered sugar. When smooth, add remaining powdered sugar a little at a time until the frosting reaches a good consistency. Add more cherry juice if needed.

To assemble: Cut each triangle horizontally from the smallest point of the triangle to the back, being careful not to cut it all the way through; it should look like an alligator's jaw. Open each "jaw," spoon frosting between each half, and spread evenly. Place top half back down and serve.

CHOCOLATE CHEESECAKE
STRAWBERRIES

Cheesecake filling:
4 oz. cream cheese
1 C. frozen whipped topping,
thawed in refrigerator
½ C. powdered sugar
1 tsp. vanilla

Strawberries:
1 pint large strawberries
1 12-oz. bag chocolate chips
Optional: Sprinkles or
mini chocolate chips for
decorating

Make the cheesecake filling by mixing the cream cheese and whipped topping until smooth. Cream in the sugar and vanilla. Cover and refrigerate while preparing the strawberries.

Melt half the chocolate chips in a glass cup or mug in the microwave for 1 minute. Stir in the remaining chocolate chips and melt in 20-second intervals until all the chocolate melts and is smooth. Do not overcook! Clean and thoroughly dry the strawberries (if they are at all wet, the water will ruin the chocolate). Dip the strawberries in the chocolate, leaving some space at the top, and place on parchment paper. If desired, sprinkle on some mini chocolate chips or sprinkles over the chocolate before it hardens. Let the chocolate completely cool and set at room temperature. Remove the stems from the strawberries and cut out the white center area. Scoop the cheesecake filling into a resealable plastic bag and seal. Cut a small hole in the corner of the bag and pipe the filling into the strawberries. Keep refrigerated until ready to serve.

CHICKEN
SATAY
with Peanut Sauce Dip

SERVES
6

Chicken Satay:
½ tsp. ground cumin
½ tsp. kosher salt
¼ tsp. ground ginger
¼ tsp. curry powder
3 chicken breasts, cut into long strips
2 T. peanut oil

Peanut Dipping Sauce:
3 T. creamy peanut butter
3 T. soy sauce
2 T. rice vinegar
1 T. honey
½ tsp. minced garlic
½ tsp. Sriracha hot sauce
¼ C. water
Chopped peanuts

Cool Cucumber Salad:
2 T. fresh chopped cilantro
6 T. rice wine vinegar
2 T. water
1 T. sugar
½ tsp. kosher salt
2 cucumbers, sliced and seeded

Chicken Satay: In a small bowl, mix spices; set aside. Toss the chicken strips in the peanut oil; stir in the spices. Cover and refrigerate 20–30 minutes. Thread onto skewers and grill.

Peanut Dipping Sauce: In a small saucepan, mix all sauce ingredients. Bring to a simmer and cook 1–2 minutes to thicken. Set aside and bring to room temperature.

Cool Cucumber Salad: Mix all ingredients but cucumbers; toss in the cucumber. Refrigerate and serve.

GRILLED
FRUIT KABOBS
with Key Lime Yogurt Dip

Fruit for kabobs:
Any melon
Strawberries
Pineapples
Mangos
Bananas
Kiwis

For basting:
Honey
Coconut flakes
Coconut white balsamic
vinegar (optional)

Yogurt dip:
1 6- to 8-oz. light yogurt (I
used Greek key lime yogurt)
¼ C. marshmallow fluff
2 oz. light cream cheese
1 tsp. lime juice or key lime
juice
Coconut flakes

Soak wooden skewers in cold water so they won't burn while on the grill. Turn on grill to medium heat. Thread each skewer with chunks of cut fruit. Warm honey in the microwave so it is warm and runny. Baste each kabob lightly with honey then sprinkle with coconut flakes. Grill until the fruit gets nice grill marks on each side. Remove to a serving plate. If desired, drizzle the kabos lightly with coconut white balsamic vinegar.

Yogurt Dip: Beat all ingredients until well blended and put in a small dish for dipping. Keep refrigerated.

SHARE YOUR FAVORITE MAY RECIPES WITH YOUR FAMILY AT THE END OF THE SECTION.

What is your favorite recipe from your grandmother?

FAVORITE FAMILY RECIPE

SERVES

_____

{ RECIPE TITLE }

Ingredients:

Instructions:

FAVORITE FAMILY RECIPE

SERVES

_____

———————————————————————————————

{ RECIPE TITLE }

Ingredients:

_____

_____

_____

_____

_____

_____

_____

_____

_____

_____

_____

_____

_____

_____

_____

_____

_____

_____

Instructions:

_____

_____

_____

_____

_____

_____

_____

_____

_____

_____

_____

_____

_____

_____

_____

_____

_____

_____

_____

_____

_____

_____

CHAPTER 6

JUNE

June

SPRING BEING A TOUGH

act to follow,

GOD CREATED JUNE.

—Al Bernstein

Dust off the grill and camping gear—summer is here! Who wants to be in the kitchen cooking all day? Not us! Summer cooking is all about the grill and light and easy meals. That doesn't mean giving up flavor—in fact, quite the contrary. Our Bacon and Blue Cheese Burgers are the most flavorful burger out there, and if you're partial to chicken on the grill, our Citrus Avocado Chicken is bursting with a fresh combination of flavors.

If you're heading to the mountains this summer, our recipe for omelets in a bag can't be beat for a quick and easy breakfast without having to make a fire. Make sure you pack the ingredients for our Walking Locos Tacos for an even easier lunch or dinner. These are both delicious recipes that require little or no clean up so you can enjoy the day hiking, playing, or relaxing with a book in a hammock.

We've also included a few desserts for fun. Our Strawberries and Cream Cake is light and refreshing. We use real strawberries in the cake and the frosting, and the resulting strawberry flavor is incredible! Elise created the recipe for our Caribbean Coconut Fudge Bars; she was inspired by a similar dessert she ordered in a little coffee shop when visiting Caneel Bay on St. John's in the Caribbean. Last but not least, you can't beat a frozen ice cream pie on a hot summer day. Our Winger's Mile-High Asphalt Pie copycat recipe combines mint chocolate chip ice cream and salted caramel on an Oreo cookie crust. It doesn't get much better than that!

RED ROBIN'S BACON AND BLUE
CHEESE BURGERS
with Creamy Buffalo Sauce
Copycat Recipe

SERVES
4

Hamburgers:
1 lb. ground beef, preferably 80/20 (leaner beef won't be as juicy)
½ C. oatmeal
1 clove garlic, minced
½ C. crumbled blue cheese
1 tsp. Worcestershire sauce
1 tsp. Frank's Original Red Hot Sauce
2 tsp. dry onion soup mix
Salt and pepper to taste

Creamy Buffalo Sauce:
¼ C. blue cheese salad dressing
¼ C. Frank's Original Red Hot Sauce

Additional ingredients:
4 hamburger buns
1 lb. thick-cut bacon, cooked
Lettuce, to taste
Blue cheese crumbles, to taste
Grilled sliced onions (optional)

In a large bowl, combine hamburger ingredients. Mix with hands until just combined. Cover and allow mixture to sit at room temperature for about 10 minutes. Form beef mixture into 4 patties and grill for approximately 4–6 minutes on each side, or until internal temperature reaches at least 155 degrees. Remove from the grill and allow the burgers to rest for 5 minutes. In the meantime, combine sauce ingredients in a small saucepan and heat until very warm but not boiling. Serve burgers on buns with additional ingredients and the Creamy Buffalo Sauce.

CITRUS AVOCADO
CHICKEN

4 skinless, boneless chicken breasts
2 ripe avocados

Salsa:
2 limes, segmented
2 oranges, segmented
1 medium grapefruit, segmented
1 serrano chile, stemmed, seeded, and minced
1 green onion, minced, white part only
1 T. finely chopped fresh basil
1 T. finely chopped fresh cilantro
1 T. honey
1 tsp. minced Anaheim chile pepper

Marinade:
2 T. citrus zest, reserved from the salsa
½ C. citrus juice, reserved from the salsa
2 T. honey
1 T. olive oil
1 tsp. minced garlic
1 serrano chile, stemmed, seeded, and minced
1 T. fresh basil, finely chopped
1 T. fresh cilantro, finely chopped
½ tsp. ground cumin

Salsa: Wash and dry limes, oranges, and grapefruit. Grate zests and set aside for use in the marinade. Peel and section citrus fruit, discard membranes, and reserve juice for the marinade. Cut each citrus segment into three or four pieces and place in a large stainless steel mixing bowl with the remaining salsa ingredients. Mix and refrigerate until 1 hour before serving.

Marinade: Whisk the reserved citrus zest and juice with remaining marinade ingredients.

Rinse chicken breasts under cold water and pat dry with paper towels. Place chicken in a large resealable plastic bag and pour in the marinade. Press out the air and seal tightly. Turn the bag to distribute the marinade. Place the bag in a bowl and refrigerate for 4–8 hours, turning occasionally.

1 hour before serving, cut the avocados into chunks. Stir avocado chunks into salsa and let sit at room temperature.

15 minutes before serving, remove chicken breasts from bag and discard the marinade. Grill the chicken breasts on medium heat for approximately 5 minutes on each side, or until juices run clear, turning the chicken only once. Let chicken rest for a few minutes before serving.

Serve grilled chicken topped with salsa.

IN A BAG
OMELET

2 eggs
1 T. water

Additional ingredient
options as desired:
Shredded cheese
Diced Ham
Bacon, cooked and crumbled
Sausage, cooked and
crumbled
Tomatoes, diced
Bell peppers, diced
Onions, diced
Mushrooms, sliced

Optional toppings:
Sour cream
Salsa
Avocado slices
Guacamole
Salt and pepper

Bring a large pot of water to a boil. While waiting for the water to boil, crack eggs into a quart-size resealable plastic freezer bag and add water. Remove air; seal. Squish the bag with hands until egg yolks are blended. Add any remaining ingredients. Press as much air out of the bag as you can and seal tightly. Squeeze the bag with hands until the ingredients are evenly distributed. Place bag in the boiling water and cook for 13 minutes, or until eggs are set. You can cook 1–6 bags at a time. To prevent plastic bag from melting, make sure the top of the bag doesn't hang out over the edge of the pot. Carefully remove bag from the water and empty eggs onto a plate. Serve with additional toppings.

SHARE YOUR FAVORITE JUNE RECIPES WITH
YOUR FAMILY AT THE END OF THE SECTION.

*Do you have a favorite recipe
for camping?*

SERVES
6

WALKING
LOCOS TACOS

6 individual-size bags Doritos
1 lb. prepared taco meat
(ground beef, ground turkey,
or shredded chicken)

Additional toppings as
desired:
Cheese, shredded
Lettuce, shredded
Tomatoes, diced
Onions, diced
Avocado slices
Guacamole
Salsa
Sour cream

Open each bag of Doritos. Crunch up the chips a little if desired. Add ¼ C. meat to chips in each bag. Add additional toppings as desired into each bag. Use a plastic fork to eat the Locos Tacos right out of the bag. No dishes to clean up!

This recipe is great for camping trips!

CHICKEN SALAD
SANDWICHES

SERVES
6

2 C. chicken, cooked and shredded

⅔ C. mayonnaise

½ tsp. onion powder

½ tsp. garlic powder

1 C. grapes, cut in half

½ C. cashews

Green leaf lettuce

Bread for sandwiches (croissants, pita pockets, tortilla wraps, sliced bread, rolls)

In a medium bowl, combine chicken, mayonnaise, onion powder, and garlic powder. If you are making the chicken salad ahead, keep chicken mixture refrigerated until ready to serve. Just before serving, stir in grapes and cashews. Spoon chicken salad mixture onto bread and add a lettuce leaf.

CALIFORNIA BREAKFAST
CASSEROLE

SERVES
12

12 frozen, precooked breakfast sausage patties, thawed

2–3 tomatoes, sliced

2–3 avocados, sliced

12 eggs

1 C. milk

1 lb. frozen hash browns, thawed

1 C. cheddar cheese, shredded

1 tsp. salt

½ tsp. pepper

Extra cheddar cheese for topping

Line the bottom of a greased 9x13 pan with sausage. Layer tomato and avocado slices over sausage. In a large bowl, beat eggs and milk. Stir in remaining ingredients. Pour egg mixture over the sausage, tomatoes, and avocados. Bake at 350 degrees for 35–45 minutes, or until set. Top with extra cheddar cheese. Serve with salsa, diced tomatoes, and sour cream if desired.

TASTY
CRAB CAKES
with Homemade Tartar Sauce

SERVES
4

½ C. mayonnaise

2 eggs

2 T. butter, melted

½ tsp. Worcestershire sauce

½ tsp. lemon juice

½ tsp. dried dill weed

¼ tsp. salt

A few dashes of cayenne pepper

½ tsp. Old Bay seasoning

16 oz. fresh crab meat

1 ½ C. panko bread crumbs, divided

Vegetable oil for frying

Homemade Tartar Sauce (see recipe below)

Homemade Tartar Sauce:

1 C. mayonnaise (Best Foods or Hellmann's)

2 T. lemon juice

2–3 T. dill pickle, finely chopped

2 tsp. dill weed, finely chopped

1/4 tsp. pepper

In a medium bowl, mix all ingredients except crab, bread crumbs, and oil until thoroughly blended. Stir in the crab meat and half of the bread crumbs. In a frying pan, heat vegetable oil over medium heat; there should be about ½ inch of oil in the bottom of the pan. Form crab cakes using about ½ C. mixture for each. Pat remaining bread crumbs on the outside of each crab cake. In hot oil, fry each crab cake until both sides are lightly browned. Remove from pan onto a plate lined with paper towels. Serve with Homemade Tartar Sauce.

Homemade Tartar Sauce: In a medium-size bowl, combine all ingredients; stir until thoroughly mixed. Chill in refrigerator for at least 1 hour. The longer you chill the sauce, the better—the flavors will get stronger with time. Stir well before serving.

SHARE YOUR FAVORITE JUNE RECIPES WITH YOUR FAMILY AT THE END OF THE SECTION.

What is your favorite recipe for a quick and easy summer meal?

WINGER'S MILE-HIGH
ASPHALT PIE
Copycat Recipe

SERVES
8

Asphalt Pie:
24 Oreos, crushed
4 T. butter, melted
1.5 quarts mint chocolate
chip ice cream, softened (ice
cream can be doubled)

Salted Caramel:
¾ C. sugar
¼ C. brown sugar
¼ C. water
4 T. unsalted butter
1 C. heavy cream, divided
½ tsp. vanilla
½ tsp. kosher salt

Whipped Cream:
1 C. whipping cream
½ C. powdered sugar

Asphalt Pie: In a mixing bowl, combine Oreos and melted butter; stir until well mixed. Press into the bottom of a pie pan. Fill pie crust with softened ice cream. Cover with plastic wrap and freeze for at least 3 hours before serving. To serve, drizzle with salted caramel and top with whipped cream

Salted Caramel: In a saucepan, heat sugars and water over medium-high heat until sugar darkens. Remove from heat; carefully whisk in butter and half the cream. Stir until smooth; add remaining cream, vanilla, and salt. This recipe makes more than is needed for pie; store the extra in an airtight container in refrigerator for up to two months.

Whipped Cream: Combine cream and sugar; whip until it forms stiff peaks.

CARIBBEAN COCONUT
FUDGE BARS

Oatmeal Crust:

1 C. flour

1 C. oatmeal

¾ C. brown sugar

½ tsp. baking soda

¼ tsp. salt

¾ C. butter, melted

Fudge:

2 C. chocolate chips

1 14-oz. can sweetened condensed milk

2 T. butter

1 tsp. vanilla

Coconut topping:

2 C. shredded coconut

⅓ C. sweetened condensed milk

Preheat oven to 350 degrees. In a medium-size bowl, combine flour, oatmeal, brown sugar, baking soda, and salt. Stir in melted butter. Press evenly into a 9 x 13 glass baking dish. Bake at 350 degrees for 8 minutes. Cool slightly. In a medium saucepan, combine all fudge ingredients. Warm over medium heat until just melted. Pour fudge over crust and allow to cool completely. In a food processor or blender, pulse coconut 2–3 times until coarsely chopped. Stir ⅓ C. sweetened condensed milk into coconut and gently spread over top of the fudge. Cool and serve.

SHARE YOUR FAVORITE JUNE RECIPES WITH YOUR FAMILY AT THE END OF THE SECTION.

What is your favorite summer dessert recipe?

SERVES
15

STRAWBERRIES AND
CREAM CAKE

Strawberry Cake:
1 C. blended fresh
strawberries*
1 box white cake mix,
unprepared
1 3-oz. box strawberry
gelatin, unprepared
1 C. canola oil
½ C. buttermilk
4 eggs

Strawberry Cream Frosting:
8 oz. cream cheese, softened
¾ C. blended fresh
strawberries*
2 C. powdered sugar
1 C. frozen whipped topping,
thawed

Preheat oven to 350 degrees. Place strawberries in blender and puree well. Set aside. In a large bowl, combine cake mix and strawberry gelatin. Stir in 1 C. blended strawberries, oil, and buttermilk. Add eggs, one at a time, mixing well after each. Pour batter into a 9 x 13 cake pan sprayed with nonstick cooking spray. Bake 30–35 minutes until toothpick comes out clean. Remove from oven and cool completely before frosting.

Strawberry Cream Frosting: In a large bowl, mix cream cheese and ¾ C. blended strawberries until smooth. Add powdered sugar. Mix well. Fold in whipped topping. Spread evenly over cooled cake. Garnish with additional fresh strawberries if desired. Refrigerate 1 hour before serving.

*One pint of fresh strawberries will be enough for both the cake and frosting.

FAVORITE FAMILY RECIPE

SERVES

_____

{ RECIPE TITLE }

Ingredients:

Instructions:

FAVORITE FAMILY RECIPE

SERVES

_____
{ RECIPE TITLE }

Ingredients:

_____
_____
_____
_____
_____
_____
_____
_____
_____
_____
_____
_____
_____
_____
_____
_____
_____
_____

Instructions:

_____
_____
_____
_____
_____
_____
_____
_____
_____
_____
_____
_____
_____
_____
_____
_____
_____

CHAPTER 7

JULY

July

SUMMER AFTERNOON—

summer afternoon;

THE TWO MOST BEAUTIFUL WORDS

in the English language.

—Henry James

No one wants to turn on the oven during the hot days of July, so most of our cooking happens on the grill. For some variety and flavor on the grill, try our Asian Glazed Pork Kabobs or Cajun Style Grill Foil Packets. And don't forget delicious salads on those warm summer evenings; you'll love our Barbecue Chicken Salad with Creamy Barbecue Dressing and our Grilled Shrimp Salad with Cilantro Verde Dressing.

The only time our oven goes on in the summer is for an irresistible dessert. To celebrate the Fourth of July, our Patriotic Poke Cake or Firecracker Sugar Cookie Bars are just the thing to eat while watching fireworks. Both can be baked when it's still cool outside in the morning and enjoyed later in the day.

As much as we all love watermelon, there always seems to be a lot of it left over after neighborhood and family summer events. Don't throw the leftovers away! Combine it with some lemon for Melonade, a refreshing summertime drink that can be sipped next to the pool on a hot summer afternoon or on the front porch on a warm summer evening.

ORANGE CREAMSICLE
PANCAKES

Pancakes:
2 C. instant pancake mix
1 1/2 C. orange juice

Cream Filling:
1 pint heavy whipping cream
1/4 C. powdered sugar
1 3-oz. pkg. instant vanilla pudding
2 T. milk

Orange Syrup:
1 12-oz. frozen orange juice concentrate
2 C. sugar
1/2 C. butter

Pancakes: Mix pancake mix and orange juice. Cook on a griddle over medium heat until pancake is golden on both sides.

Cream Filling: In a large mixer, beat cream until stiff peaks form. It should be very thick. Whip in the powdered sugar and then the instant pudding. If needed, add milk to make the consistency a little creamier.

Orange Syrup: In a small saucepan, combine all ingredients and bring to a boil, stirring occasionally. Remove from heat and serve.

To serve, sandwich a large dollop of the vanilla cream between two pancakes; drizzle orange syrup over the top.

L & L BARBECUE AUTHENTIC HAWAIIAN
MACARONI SALAD
Copycat Recipe

SERVES
8

1 lb. macaroni

2 T. apple cider vinegar

2 carrots, shredded

¼ C. onion, shredded (optional)

2 ½ C. Best Foods or Hellman's mayonnaise (no substitutes!)

¼ C. milk

2 tsp. sugar

Kosher salt and pepper, to taste

Cook macaroni according to package directions. Drain well and place in a large bowl. While macaroni is still hot, sprinkle with vinegar, carrot, and onion. Toss until well combined. Allow to cool for 10–15 minutes. In a separate smaller bowl, whisk mayonnaise, milk, and sugar. Fold mayonnaise mixture into the macaroni until all noodles are evenly coated. Add salt and pepper to taste. Cover and refrigerate at least 4 hours (best if overnight). Gently stir before serving, adding a little more milk if the salad seems dry.

SHARE YOUR FAVORITE JULY RECIPES WITH YOUR FAMILY AT THE END OF THE SECTION.

Do you have a favorite side dish recipe for a neighborhood or church barbecue?

FIRECRACKER SUGAR
COOKIE BARS

⅔ C. shortening or butter, softened

1 C. sugar

2 eggs

⅓ C. milk

1 tsp. vanilla

3 C. flour

2 tsp. baking powder

1 tsp. salt

Cream Cheese Frosting:

8 oz. cream cheese, softened

¼ C. butter, softened

1 tsp. vanilla

1–1½ lbs. powdered sugar

Toppings:

4 packets red and blue Pop Rocks candy

Edible star sprinkles (optional)

Preheat oven to 350 degrees. Combine shortening (or butter) and sugar; beat. Add eggs, milk, and vanilla, and beat to combine. In a separate bowl, combine flour, baking powder, and salt. Slowly add dry ingredients to wet ingredients. Mix until dough holds together in a ball. Spray a 9 x 13 glass baking dish with nonstick cooking spray.

Drop spoonfuls of dough evenly around pan. Press dough down evenly with hands or spatula. Bake 15–18 minutes or until dough barely starts turning light brown around the edges. Do not overbake! Cool to room temperature before frosting. For frosting, beat cream cheese, butter, and vanilla until well mixed. Add powdered sugar to desired consistency. Spread frosting over cooled cookie bars. Cut cookies into squares and top with Pop Rocks candy and sprinkles. Serve chilled.

PATRIOTIC
POKE CAKE

Cake:
1 box white cake mix,
unprepared
½ C. water
½ C. sour cream
⅓ C. vegetable oil
3 eggs

Filling:
1 3-oz. pkg. raspberry or
strawberry Jell-O gelatin
1 3-oz. pkg. berry blue Jell-O
gelatin
Water (see instructions)

Frosting:
8 oz. cream cheese
½ C. sugar
12 oz. frozen whipped
topping, thawed

Optional:
Raspberries, strawberries, or
blueberries
Sprinkles

Preheat oven to 350 degrees. Mix cake ingredients and bake in a 9 x 13 pan according to directions on the cake mix box. Allow cake to cool completely. Mix contents of the first Jell-O package with 1 C. boiling water, then stir in ½ C. cold water. The Jell-O mix needs to remain liquid, so don't refrigerate. Poke a bunch of holes in the cake using the handle end of a wooden spoon. Using a child's medicine dispenser, put 1–2 tsp. of Jell-O in every other hole. When finished, repeat steps with the second color of Jell-O. Cover cake and refrigerate until ready to serve. For frosting, beat cream cheese and sugar until smooth and fold in whipped topping. Spread evenly over cooled cake. If desired, top with fresh berries or sprinkles.

BARBECUE
CHICKEN SALAD
with Creamy Barbecue Dressing

SERVES
6

3 chicken breasts

1 ½ C. barbecue sauce, divided

3 hearts of romaine, chopped

1 C. frozen corn, thawed

1 can black beans, drained and rinsed

6 green onions, chopped

2 C. cheddar cheese, shredded

2 C. tortilla chips, crushed into pieces

Creamy Barbecue Dressing:

1 C. mayonnaise

⅓ C. milk

⅓ C. buttermilk

2 T. fresh cilantro, finely chopped

1 T. lime juice

1 tsp. white vinegar

1 tsp. granulated sugar

1 clove garlic, finely minced

½ tsp. salt

⅛ tsp. cayenne pepper

⅛ tsp. black pepper

¼ tsp. ground cumin

¼–½ C. barbecue sauce

Combine chicken and 1 C. barbecue sauce in a resealable plastic bag. Seal tightly and refrigerate for at least an hour. Remove chicken from bag, discard marinade, and grill chicken until cooked through. Use remaining barbecue sauce to baste chicken while grilling. When internal temperature of chicken reaches 165 degrees, remove from grill and set aside to rest. In a large serving bowl, toss romaine with corn, black beans, and green onions. Slice chicken and add it to the top of the salad. Top with shredded cheese and tortilla chips. Serve with Creamy Barbecue Dressing.

Dressing: Combine all ingredients and whisk vigorously until smooth. Ingredients can also be blended in a blender. Refrigerate dressing until ready to serve.

SHARE YOUR FAVORITE JULY RECIPES WITH YOUR FAMILY AT THE END OF THE SECTION.

What is your favorite recipe for cooking on the grill?

GRILLED
SHRIMP SALAD
with Cilantro Verde Dressing

SERVES
6

1 lb. shrimp, uncooked, with tails on
1 T. Cajun seasoning
4 C. leafy green lettuce or spinach
1 red pepper
Feta or gorgonzola cheese
Cherry tomatoes
Cilantro Verde Dressing (see recipe below)

Cilantro Verde Dressing:
1 C. bottled salsa verde (preferably Herdez brand)
1 0.4-oz. packet buttermilk ranch dressing mix
⅓ C. chopped fresh cilantro
⅓ C. sour cream
⅓ C. plain Greek yogurt
1 T. fresh lime juice
1 T. sugar
1 tsp. minced garlic
½ tsp. kosher salt
¼ tsp. cumin
Dash of Tabasco sauce

Rinse the shrimp in cold water and pat dry with a paper towel. Place shrimp into a large resealable plastic bag and add the Cajun seasoning. Toss to coat. Warm a little oil in a small frying pan. Dice the red pepper and sauté in the frying pan until it begins to soften. Grill the shrimp over medium heat; it only needs a few minutes on each side. Shrimp should be pink and cooked through. Place lettuce in individual bowls and top with the roasted red peppers, cheese, tomatoes, and grilled shrimp. Drizzle with Cilantro Verde Dressing.

Cilantro Verde Dressing: Combine all ingredients in a blender and blend until smooth. Keep refrigerated.

ASIAN GLAZED
PORK KABOBS

SERVES
8

4 lbs. boneless pork chops, thick cut

Marinade Ingredients:
¾ C. sugar
½ C. soy sauce
3 T. hoisin sauce
2 T. dry sherry
1 T. minced fresh ginger
2 tsp minced garlic

Cut the pork chops into bite-size pieces. Discard excess fat. In a medium bowl, mix all marinade ingredients. Stir in the pork chop pieces and cover. Marinate for at least an hour—the longer, the better. Thread the pork onto skewers but don't throw the marinade away. Allow the uncooked kabobs to sit at room temperature for about 20 minutes. In the meantime, pour the excess marinade into a saucepan over medium high heat and bring to a boil for a full minute; reduce to low heat. Grill the kabobs over medium heat, basting generously with the marinade every couple of minutes until fully cooked. Serve with a side of fresh, grilled pineapple.

CAJUN-STYLE GRILL
FOIL PACKETS

4 ears corn on the cob, cut in half or thirds

4 red potatoes, washed and cubed

20–30 uncooked shrimp, peeled and deveined

1 lb. smoked sausage, cut into chunks

Melted butter or olive oil, to taste

½ C. chicken broth

Cajun/Creole seasoning, to taste (preferably Tony Chachere's brand)

Salt and pepper to taste

Heat grill to 400 degrees; you can use the oven preheated to 400 degrees. Evenly distribute corn, potatoes, shrimp, and sausage between 4 heavy-duty foil sheets (about 12 x 18 inches each). Drizzle melted butter and 2 T. chicken broth over each foil packet. Season evenly and generously with Cajun seasoning, salt, and pepper. Tightly seal foil packets by folding up the sides over the contents and tightly folding up the ends over the seam. Grill 30–40 minutes or until potatoes are tender, flipping once halfway through. Be careful opening the packets when you check for doneness as the steam inside is very hot!

REFRESHING
MELONADE

SERVES
8
CUPS

5 C. pureed watermelon

3 C. cold water

1 C. sugar

2 T. True Lemon or ¾ C. lemon juice

Dice watermelon and remove all black seeds (white seeds are fine). Puree diced watermelon in a blender until smooth. Measure out 5 C. watermelon puree into a large pitcher. Add water, sugar, and lemon. Stir well and refrigerate. Makes 2 quarts.

SHARE YOUR FAVORITE JULY RECIPES WITH YOUR FAMILY AT THE END OF THE SECTION.

Do you have a recipe for a favorite lemonade or other summertime drink?

EASY
FRUIT PIZZA

Sugar Cookie Pizza Crust:
½ C. butter, softened
½ C. sugar
½ C. brown sugar
2 eggs
1 tsp. vanilla
1 tsp. baking powder
1 tsp. salt
2 ½ C. flour

Frosting Layer:
1 8-oz. pkg. cream cheese
1 C. powdered sugar

Fruit Toppings:
Apples
Bananas
Blueberries
Grapes
Kiwi Fruit
Mango chunks
Peaches
Raspberries
Strawberries

Sugar Cookie Pizza Crust: Cream butter and sugars. Mix in eggs and vanilla and beat well. Add dry ingredients. Form dough into a large ball and wrap in plastic wrap. Refrigerate for 1 hour. Roll dough out in a large circle with a rolling pin. Gently place on a pizza pan or stone sprayed with nonstick cooking spray. Bake at 375 degrees for 12–15 minutes. Remove from oven when edges and top start to lightly brown. Let cool completely.

Frosting: Combine cream cheese and powdered sugar; mix until smooth. If you want a sweeter frosting, add more powdered sugar. Spread on cooled sugar cookie crust.

Fruit Toppings: Wash and slice fresh fruit. Creatively arrange fruit on top of frosting.

FAVORITE FAMILY RECIPE

SERVES

___

_____

{ RECIPE TITLE }

Ingredients:

_____

_____

_____

_____

_____

_____

_____

_____

_____

_____

_____

_____

_____

_____

_____

_____

_____

_____

Instructions:

_____

_____

_____

_____

_____

_____

_____

_____

_____

_____

_____

_____

_____

_____

_____

_____

_____

_____

_____

_____

_____

_____

FAVORITE FAMILY RECIPE

SERVES
—

_____
{ RECIPE TITLE }

Ingredients:

_____

_____

_____

_____

_____

_____

_____

_____

_____

_____

_____

_____

_____

_____

_____

_____

Instructions:

_____

_____

_____

_____

_____

_____

_____

_____

_____

_____

_____

_____

_____

_____

_____

_____

CHAPTER 8

AUGUST

August

IT'S DIFFICULT TO THINK

anything but pleasant thoughts

WHILE EATING A

homegrown tomato.

—Lewis Grizzard

Homegrown tomatoes. Corn on the cob. Squash and zucchini. These are the foods we look forward to in August. If you have your own garden or access to a farmer's market, you've got to try our Homemade Canned Spaghetti Sauce and our Fresh Homemade Salsa. The fresh, garden tomatoes make all the difference! When you or your neighbors are overflowing with zucchini, our Parmesan Squash and Zucchini Bake recipe is a delicious and healthy way to enjoy the benefits of this versatile squash.

The school year starts up again for most of us in August. It's back to early-morning breakfasts and packing lunches. Our grab-and-go make-ahead McDonald's Breakfast Yogurt Parfaits make the morning go smoother, and our Zesty Italian Wraps are a nice break from a PB&J in the lunch box. For the first day of school, have some warm Oatmeal Butterscotch Cookies ready to come out of the oven when the kids come home. Invite the neighbor kids over too and enjoy listening to the adventures from the first day of school!

MCDONALD'S BREAKFAST
YOGURT PARFAITS
Copycat Recipe

3 ⅓ C. strawberries, raspberries, blackberries, and/or blueberries (fresh or frozen)

32 oz. plain or vanilla Greek yogurt

2 ½ C. granola

5 16-oz. clear plastic cups

5 snack-size resealable plastic bags

Place ⅓ C. berries in the bottom of each 16-oz. clear cup. Spoon ⅓ C. yogurt on top of the berries. Repeat layers. Fill each plastic bag with ½ C. granola and seal (one for each cup). Cover each cup tightly with plastic wrap and seal with rubber band. Place or tie a granola bag on each cup along with a plastic spoon. Store in refrigerator for up to 5 days.

EASY
CHICKEN FLAUTAS

1 ½ C. chicken, shredded

6 oz. cream cheese

1 C. Monterey Jack cheese, shredded

⅓ C. salsa

Salt and pepper to taste

8 flour tortillas

Preheat oven to 400 degrees. In a medium-size bowl, combine chicken, cream cheese, Monterey Jack cheese, salsa, salt, and pepper. Mix well. Evenly distribute chicken mixture among tortillas, making a line down the middle of each tortilla and then rolling each up tightly. Line a baking sheet with aluminum foil and spray with nonstick cooking spray. Place rolled-up tortillas evenly spaced on the cookie sheet (seam side down) and spray cooking spray generously over the top. Bake for 10–12 minutes or until tortillas become golden brown. Serve flautas with salsa, guacamole, and/or sour cream.

ZESTY
ITALIAN WRAPS

6 slices deli ham

6 slices salami

12 pepperoni slices

2 provolone cheese slices

2 lettuce leaves

Banana peppers

2 flour tortillas

Zesty Italian dressing

Divide and layer meats, cheese slices, lettuce leaves, and banana peppers on the two tortillas. Lightly drizzle dressing over peppers and lettuce. Roll the wraps up tightly. Cut each wrap in half and wrap in plastic wrap. Keep refrigerated until ready to serve. Serve with Italian dressing.

SHARE YOUR FAVORITE AUGUST RECIPES WITH YOUR FAMILY AT THE END OF THE SECTION.

What is your favorite sandwich or wrap recipe?

OATMEAL BUTTERSCOTCH
COOKIES

1 C. butter

1 C. granulated sugar

1 C. brown sugar firmly packed

2 eggs

1 tsp. vanilla

1 ½ C. flour

1 tsp. baking soda

1 tsp. salt

1 tsp. cinnamon

3 ½ C. old-fashioned oats or quick-cooking oats

1 11-oz. bag butterscotch chips, approximately 1 ¾ C.

Preheat oven to 350 degrees. In a large bowl or electric mixer, blend butter, sugar, and brown sugar. Add eggs and vanilla; beat until creamy and smooth. In a separate bowl, whisk flour, baking soda, salt, and cinnamon. Add the dry mixture to the butter/sugar mixture and blend well. Mix in the oats. Stir in the butterscotch chips. Roll dough into 1-inch balls and place evenly on a lightly greased cookie sheet (nonstick cooking spray works best to grease the cookie sheet). Bake for 10 minutes, or until the edges of the cookies are lightly browned. Place on cooling rack.

To freeze cookies: Allow cookies to cool completely. Place cookies in an airtight container or resealable freezer bag. Freeze for up to 2 months.

SHARE YOUR FAVORITE AUGUST RECIPES WITH YOUR FAMILY AT THE END OF THE SECTION.

What is your favorite cookie recipe?

FIVE-MINUTE
CREAMY CORN DIP

SERVES
10

2 15-oz. cans Mexi-corn, drained

2 10-oz, cans Rotel tomatoes with green chiles, drained

1 ½ C. Greek yogurt

½ C. mayonnaise

1 ½ C. shredded cheddar cheese (reserve some for garnish)

1 1-oz. pkg. dry ranch dressing mix

1 bunch green onions, chopped (reserve some for garnish)

Salt and pepper to taste

In a large bowl, combine all ingredients and stir gently until combined. Refrigerate dip until ready to serve. Garnish with reserved cheddar cheese and green onions. Serve with corn tortilla chips.

FRESH HOMEMADE
SALSA

6–8 fresh tomatoes, peeled and diced (or 3 cans diced tomatoes)

1 small can diced jalapeño peppers (more or less depending on how spicy you like it)

3 T. lime juice

1 tsp. red wine vinegar

1 tsp. salt

2 tsp. minced garlic

2 tsp. cumin

2 tsp. paprika

1 tsp. chili powder

½ bunch cilantro

1 green onion, diced

In a food processor, combine all ingredients except green onion. Pulse the food processor a few times until everything is diced but is not completely blended. Pour salsa into a medium-size bowl and stir in the onion. Cover and refrigerate at least 3 hours or overnight to let flavors blend. Serve with tortilla chips.

SNICKERS
APPLE SALAD

SERVES
8

6 crisp apples

4 full-size Snickers candy bars

1 8-oz. container frozen whipped topping, thawed

Cut apples into bite-size pieces. Dice Snickers bars into bite-size pieces. In a medium-size bowl, mix cut-up Snickers bars and apples. Fold in whipped topping. Cover and refrigerate until ready to serve.

HOMEMADE CANNED
SPAGHETTI SAUCE

25 lbs. tomatoes

4 large red bell peppers

1 large green bell pepper

5 onions

4 6-oz. cans tomato paste

¼ C. soy sauce

3 T. Worcestershire sauce

⅔ C. packed brown sugar

¼ C. salt

10 cloves garlic, chopped or minced

3 T. dried oregano

3 T. dried basil

2 tsp. red pepper flakes

2 bay leaves

1 ¼ C. lemon juice, for jars

Fill a large pot or Dutch oven halfway with water; bring to a boil. Using a slotted spoon, add tomatoes one at a time until you can't fit any more (about 8–10 tomatoes). Boil for 1–2 minutes. Remove tomatoes one at a time with a slotted spoon and plunge in an ice-water bath. Peel and quarter tomatoes. In a food processor, cover and process green peppers and onions in batches until finely chopped. To add extra flavor, sauté the peppers and onions in a little oil and with a pinch of salt before processing. In a large stockpot, combine the tomatoes (do not discard excess juices from the tomatoes), onion/pepper mixture, tomato paste, soy sauce, Worcestershire sauce, brown sugar, salt, garlic, oregano, basil, pepper flakes, and bay leaves. For a thick and smooth sauce, use an immersion blender to blend the tomatoes until smooth with no large chunks. You can also blend it in batches in a blender. Bring to a boil. Reduce heat. Simmer uncovered for 4–5 hours, stirring every 15 minutes or so. Discard bay leaves.

Put 2 T. lemon juice in each of 9 or 10 hot 1-quart jars. Ladle hot mixture into jars, leaving ½-inch headspace at the top. Remove air bubbles. Wipe rims and adjust lids. Process for 40 minutes in a boiling-water canner.

NOTE: The processing time listed is for altitudes of 1,000 feet or less. For altitudes up to 3,000 feet, add 5 minutes; up to 6,000 feet, add 10 minutes; up to 8,000 feet, add 15 minutes; up to 10,000 feet, add 20 minutes.

PARMESAN SQUASH AND
ZUCCHINI BAKE

SERVES
8-10

1 T. olive oil

2 medium-size yellow squash, sliced lengthwise and cut into ¼-inch slices (about 4 C.)

2 medium-size zucchini squash, sliced lengthwise and cut into ¼-inch slices (about 4 C.)

1 T. minced garlic

1 T. fresh thyme leaves or ½ tsp. dried thyme

2 tomatoes, sliced

2 eggs

⅓ C. light sour cream

1 C. crumbled feta, not tightly packed

2 T. Parmesan cheese, grated

1 T. lemon juice

Salt and pepper to taste

Preheat oven to 375 degrees and spray a large casserole dish with nonstick spray. Heat oil in a large nonstick frying pan. Add the squash, garlic, and thyme. Sauté and stir until the squash is just starting to soften slightly. Don't overcook! Remove from heat and add tomatoes. In a medium-size bowl, beat eggs, sour cream, cheeses, and lemon juice. Place half the squash in the bottom of a casserole dish. Sprinkle with salt and pepper. Spread ½ of the egg mixture over the squash. Repeat with remaining squash-and-egg mixture. Top with additional feta and Parmesan cheese if desired. Bake for 40–45 minutes. The mixture should be bubbling and slightly set. Serve hot.

SHARE YOUR FAVORITE AUGUST RECIPES WITH YOUR FAMILY AT THE END OF THE SECTION.

Do you have a favorite way to prepare your garden vegetables?

RASPBERRY
PEACH COBBLER

8–10 fresh peaches (can use canned or frozen peaches)

1 ½ C. raspberries, fresh or frozen

1 3-oz. peach or raspberry Jell-O gelatin mix

1 box white cake mix, unprepared

¼ C. butter, melted

¼ C. water

Preheat oven to 350 degrees. Layer peaches on the bottom of a 9 x 13 pan; use enough peaches to fill the pan half full. Place raspberries evenly over top of peaches. Sprinkle Jell-O gelatin mix over peaches and raspberries. Carefully sprinkle dry cake mix over the Jell-O layer. Drizzle butter and water evenly over the cake mix. Place in oven and bake for 45 minutes, or until cake layer is lightly browned. Serve warm with ice cream or whipped cream.

FAVORITE FAMILY RECIPE

SERVES

{ RECIPE TITLE }

Ingredients:

Instructions:

FAVORITE FAMILY RECIPE

SERVES

{ RECIPE TITLE }

Ingredients:

Instructions:

CHAPTER 9

SEPTEMBER

September

BY ALL THESE LOVELY TOKENS,

September days are here,

WITH SUMMER'S BEST OF WEATHER

and autumn's best of cheer.

—H. H. Jackson

With school in full swing, it's time to once again gather the family for a healthy, home-cooked dinner each night. After the "lazy days" and vacations of summer, this can be a bit of a challenge. We can become slaves to schedules again in September with homework, fall sports, and other activities. With all of these changes, it is more important than ever to have some time to unwind over a good meal with the family. It gives everyone the opportunity to share the good and bad experiences of the day.

Our favorite recipes in September center around meals that are warm and comforting as well as easy to prepare. Casseroles, one-pot meals, and slow-cooker meals are just the ticket! Our Easy Slow-Cooker Pork Chops, One-Pot Chicken Teriyaki Rice Bowls, and Cheesy Chicken and Rice Casserole are easy and delicious meals to serve this time of year.

Let's not forget the apple harvest! Our mom was raised on an apple orchard in Washington State. While apples picked right off the tree are pretty hard to beat, we have a few apple recipes here that you've got to try—and that will make you want apples for much more than just apple pie. Our Apple Dumplings and Yummy Apple Fries with Caramel Cream Dip are two apple desserts everyone loves this time of year. And if you thought a grilled cheese sandwich couldn't get any better, throw in some apples along with some ham slices and brie cheese to enjoy an Apple, Ham, and Cheddar Melt Sandwich that is loaded with flavor.

CHEESY CHICKEN AND RICE
CASSEROLE

SERVES
6

2 C. long-grain white rice, uncooked

1 ½ C. shredded cheddar cheese, divided

½ tsp. salt

1 tsp. pepper

6 boneless, skinless, chicken breast halves

2 10.5-oz. cans cream of chicken soup, undiluted

3 C. water

1 env. dry onion soup mix

Preheat oven to 350 degrees. Spray 9 x 13 baking pan with nonstick cooking spray. Layer rice, 1 C. cheese, salt, and pepper in pan. Place chicken breasts on top. Place rounded spoonfuls of cream of chicken soup over the chicken breasts and rice. Pour water on top and sprinkle with onion soup mix. Bake uncovered for 1 ½ hours, checking water after 1 hour. If water is absorbed before chicken and rice are completely cooked, you can add an additional ½ C. water to keep casserole moist. Remove casserole from oven and stir excess sauce into the rice. Sprinkle remaining ½ C. cheese on top.

EASY SLOW-COOKER
PORK CHOPS

SERVES
6

6–8 pork chops, thinly sliced

1 env. Hidden Valley Ranch Dressing Mix

1 can cream of chicken soup

1 can cream of mushroom soup

Spray slow-cooker with nonstick cooking spray. Put pork chops in slow-cooker. Sprinkle ranch dressing powder evenly over the pork. Cover with soups. Cook on low 6–8 hours or on high 3–4 hours.

Serve with mashed potatoes or rice.

PLANET HOLLYWOOD
CAP'N CRUNCH
CHICKEN
Copycat Recipe

SERVES
4

2 boneless, skinless chicken breasts
1 C. buttermilk
1 egg
2 C. Cap'n Crunch cereal
½ C. panko bread crumbs
½ C. Wondra flour
½ tsp. onion powder
½ tsp. garlic powder
½ tsp. salt
¼ tsp. white pepper
Vegetable oil for frying

Creole Mustard Sauce:
2 T. Grey Poupon Dijon mustard
3 T. mayonnaise

Honey Mustard Sauce:
2 T. yellow mustard
2 T. honey

Pound each chicken breast flat and cut lengthwise into 5–6 long slices. Place in a bowl. Cover with buttermilk; marinate overnight. Before breading, mix egg into the buttermilk marinade. Using a food processor, crush the Cap'n Crunch cereal into crumbs; you can also put the cereal in a plastic bag and crush with a rolling pin. In a medium bowl, combine the cereal, bread crumbs, flour, onion powder, garlic powder, salt, and pepper. Remove chicken from buttermilk and completely coat it with the dry mixture. Discard leftover buttermilk. Heat oil in a frying pan and fry the chicken for 4–6 minutes or until golden brown and crispy. Remove to paper towels or a rack to drain. Serve hot with chilled Creole Mustard Sauce or Honey Mustard Sauce.

ONE-POT CHICKEN TERIYAKI
RICE BOWLS

SERVES
6

1 lb. chicken, cut into 1-inch
pieces
3 T. teriyaki sauce
2 C. long-grain white rice,
uncooked
3 ½ C. water
Kosher salt to taste
¼ C. teriyaki sauce
3 T. soy sauce
½ C. carrots, chopped
⅓ C. green onion, chopped
⅓ C. peas, optional
1 C. broccoli, chopped
Teriyaki sauce to taste

In a large, deep skillet, cook chicken over medium-high heat in 3 T. teriyaki sauce until just white on the outside; it doesn't need to be cooked through. Add remaining ingredients except broccoli and extra teriyaki sauce; bring to a boil. Reduce heat and cover with lid. Simmer for about 20 minutes. Add broccoli, cover again, and simmer an additional 5 minutes or until rice is cooked through. Spoon extra teriyaki sauce to taste over the rice and serve immediately.

INSTANT POT SUNDAY
POT ROAST

3 lbs. beef chuck roast

Salt to taste

4 T. olive oil, divided

2 C. beef broth

1 white or yellow onion, quartered

1 lb. baby potatoes

1 C. baby carrots

1 env. dry onion soup mix

Sprinkle pot roast with salt and set aside. Add 2 T. olive oil to Instant Pot and set to sauté. When oil becomes hot and shimmery, add pot roast and sear for 4–5 minutes on each side. Add beef broth. In a gallon-size resealable plastic bag, combine vegetables, 2 T. olive oil, and onion soup mix. Shake until vegetables are evenly coated. Put veggies in Instant pot and distribute evenly around roast. Place lid on Instant Pot with steam valve closed. Switch Instant Pot setting to manual and set for 60–80 minutes on high pressure, depending on size of your roast. Natural-release steam for at least 10 minutes, then quick-release steam. Remove roast from Instant Pot. Slice and serve with vegetables. Use extra drippings from the Instant Pot to make gravy.

SHARE YOUR FAVORITE SEPTEMBER RECIPES WITH YOUR FAMILY AT THE END OF THE SECTION.

Do you have a favorite comfort food meal?

HARVEST
PEAR SALAD
with Cranberry Vinaigrette Dressing

8 C. spring mix bagged salad
2 fresh pears, sliced
Pumpkin spiced pecans (see instructions below)
1 C. feta cheese crumbles
1 C. dried cranberries

Pumpkin Spiced Pecans:
¼ C. sugar
1 tsp. pumpkin pie spice
1 C. whole pecans

Cranberry Vinaigrette Dressing:
1 C. fresh cranberries
⅓ C. orange juice
⅓ C. sugar
¼ C. olive oil
1 T. red wine vinegar
1 tsp. salt

Salad: Layer all ingredients and toss with Cranberry Vinaigrette Dressing. Start with a small amount of dressing and add more to taste.

Pumpkin Spiced Pecans: In a small bowl, mix sugar and pumpkin pie spice until blended well. In a small skillet, combine sugar mixture and pecans; heat on medium until sugar melts, stirring constantly. Be careful not to burn the sugar. As soon as sugar melts onto the pecans, spoon pecans onto aluminum foil to cool.

Cranberry Vinaigrette Dressing: In a medium saucepan, combine cranberries, orange juice, and sugar. Cook on medium-high heat, stirring constantly, until all the cranberries pop. Simmer for about 5 minutes. Pour cranberry mixture into a blender and add olive oil, vinegar, and salt. Blend until smooth. The dressing will be thick and creamy. If you prefer a thinner dressing, add small amounts of water (1 T. at a time) until it reaches the desired consistency. Refrigerate until ready to serve.

APPLE, HAM, AND CHEDDAR MELT
SANDWICHES

SERVES
2

2 slices artisan bread
Brie cheese, to taste
¼ lb. maple or honey ham, sliced very thin
2 T. apple butter
1 Gala apple, sliced thin (Fuji or Pink Lady apples are also good)
2 slices sharp cheddar cheese
Butter for grilling

Spread Brie cheese evenly over one slice of bread. On that same slice, layer ham, apple butter, apples, and cheddar cheese. Top with remaining slice of bread. Spread butter over the outside of the sandwich and grill in a skillet over medium-low heat as if making a grilled-cheese sandwich. Slice in half and serve hot.

SHARE YOUR FAVORITE SEPTEMBER RECIPES WITH YOUR FAMILY AT THE END OF THE SECTION.
What is your favorite recipe to make on a busy night?

GRILLED CHICKEN
PASTA PRIMAVERA

1 pkg. Good Seasons Italian dressing mix
¼ C. olive oil
½ C. balsamic vinegar
3 chicken breasts
2 tsp. fresh minced garlic
3 medium tomatoes, diced
1 crookneck yellow squash, diced
½ C. chicken broth
2 tsp. chicken bouillon
Salt and pepper to taste
¼ C. fresh basil, chopped
Mozzarella cheese
Parmesan cheese
1 lb. angel hair pasta or thin spaghetti noodles

At least 2 hours before serving, make marinade by combining Italian dressing mix, olive oil, and balsamic vinegar in gallon-size resealable plastic bag or large bowl. Cut each chicken breast into two thin halves and place in marinade. Refrigerate.

Thirty minutes before serving, remove chicken from marinade and grill over medium heat. When fully cooked, slice into long strips. Meanwhile, in a large frying pan over medium heat, sauté minced garlic in oil. Add diced tomatoes, squash, chicken broth, chicken bouillon, salt, and pepper. Simmer about 20 minutes, or until squash is fully cooked; remove from heat and toss in fresh basil. While simmering, cook pasta according to package directions. Layer individual bowls with noodles, a scoop of the tomato-squash sauce, and sliced grilled chicken. Top with mozzarella and Parmesan cheeses.

ROASTED BUTTERNUT SQUASH
FLATBREAD PIZZA

2 C. butternut squash, cut into squares
2 C. kale, cut into small pieces
2–3 T. butter
1 tsp. minced garlic
4 naan flatbreads
Mozzarella cheese, shredded
1 C. bacon, cooked and crumbled
Parmesan cheese, shredded

Place the cut butternut squash squares on a roasting pan sprayed with nonstick cooking spray. Bake at 375 degrees for 20–30 minutes or until the squash starts to soften and look roasted along the edges. Watch it closely; the roasting time required depends on the size the squares are cut.

In a small frying pan with a drop of oil, sauté the kale pieces until they soften slightly and turn a vibrant green color. In a small dish, melt the butter and garlic in the microwave for about 45 seconds. Place individual flatbreads on a cookie sheet. Brush each flatbread with the melted garlic butter. Sprinkle on a layer of Mozzarella then top that with crumbled bacon, cooked kale pieces, roasted butternut squash, and Parmesan cheese sprinkled over everything. Bake at 375 degrees, just until cheese melts. It should only take about 5 minutes.

APPLE
DUMPLINGS

2 Granny Smith apples

2 8-oz. cans crescent rolls

1 C. butter

1 C. sugar

1 tsp. vanilla

1 12-oz. can Sprite or

Mountain Dew

Cinnamon to taste

Peel and core apples and cut each into 8 slices. Roll each apple slice in a crescent roll. Place in a 9 x 13 baking pan sprayed with nonstick cooking spray. Melt butter in a large bowl; add sugar and stir. Stir in vanilla and pour entire mixture over the wrapped apples. Pour Sprite or Mountain Dew around the edges of the pan. Sprinkle with cinnamon and bake at 350 degrees for 40 minutes. Serve with vanilla ice cream and sauce from the pan.

YUMMY
APPLE FRIES
with Caramel Cream Dip

Apples:

Vegetable oil for frying

1 C. buttermilk

1 C. sugar

4–5 tart, crisp apples (Pink Lady or Granny Smith)

Wondra flour

Cinnamon and sugar to taste

Dip:

8 oz. cream cheese

8 oz. frozen whipped topping, thawed

1 C. caramel sauce

In a frying pan or deep fryer, heat vegetable oil for frying. In a medium bowl, mix buttermilk and sugar. Peel and slice apples and add them to the buttermilk mixture as you go to prevent browning. In a shallow dish, put a layer of Wondra flour; pull the apples out of the buttermilk mixture one at a time, and lightly coat all sides in the flour. When oil is hot, gently place coated apples into the oil; they should not touch. When the bottom side begins to turn golden, flip over and brown the second side. Quickly remove to a tray lined with paper towels to soak up excess grease; cool. Sprinkle apples with cinnamon and sugar while they are hot.

Dip: Mix cream cheese and whipped topping until completely blended then stir in caramel sauce. Place into a bowl for dipping. Drizzle a little extra caramel sauce over the top.

SHARE YOUR FAVORITE SEPTEMBER RECIPES WITH YOUR FAMILY AT THE END OF THE SECTION.

Do you have a favorite apple dessert recipe?

FAVORITE FAMILY RECIPE

SERVES

_____

{ RECIPE TITLE }

Ingredients:

_____
_____
_____
_____
_____
_____
_____
_____
_____
_____
_____
_____
_____
_____
_____
_____
_____
_____

Instructions:

_____
_____
_____
_____
_____
_____
_____
_____
_____
_____
_____
_____
_____
_____
_____
_____
_____
_____
_____

FAVORITE FAMILY RECIPE

SERVES

_____
{ RECIPE TITLE }

Ingredients:

_____
_____
_____
_____
_____
_____
_____
_____
_____
_____
_____
_____
_____
_____
_____
_____
_____
_____
_____

Instructions:

_____
_____
_____
_____
_____
_____
_____
_____
_____
_____
_____
_____
_____
_____
_____
_____
_____
_____

CHAPTER 10

OCTOBER

October

I'M SO GLAD

I live in a world

WHERE THERE ARE

Octobers.

—L. M. Montgomery, *Anne of Green Gables*

Bring on the fall! There's a chill in the air, the leaves are changing colors, and pumpkins dot the fields. Our favorite recipes this time of year shift to warm soups and anything pumpkin. We even love pumpkin drinks! Our cold Wizarding World of Harry Potter Pumpkin Juice and our hot Pumpkin Steamers are both included here. And with Halloween coming up at the end of the month, we are always on the lookout for a new and fun Halloween treat!

A favorite tradition this time of year is to gather friends and family for a night of trick-or-treating on Halloween. Soup in a Pumpkin is often on the menu. How fun is it to cook a delicious soup right in a pumpkin! The kids love it and it gives them a hot, hearty meal before filling their tummies with treats.

Another favorite thing to do in October is to gather to carve pumpkins. We never throw out the pumpkin seeds; they can be the best treat of all! Our Sweet and Spicy Pumpkin Seeds are addicting. Once you eat one, you can't stop popping them in your mouth.

PUMPKIN
PANCAKES
with Caramel Maple Syrup

SERVES
6

Candied Pecans:
½ C. chopped pecans
3 T. brown sugar
Sprinkle of cinnamon

Pancakes:
2 C. dry pancake mix
2 T. brown sugar
1 tsp. pumpkin pie spice
1 ½ C. water
½ C. pumpkin puree

Caramel Maple Syrup:
1 C. brown sugar
1 C. whipping cream
1 C. white corn syrup
½ tsp. Mapleine maple flavoring
Sprinkle of cinnamon

In a small frying pan over medium heat, cook the chopped pecans, brown sugar, and cinnamon over medium heat until sugar melts and coats the pecans. Remove from heat and spread into a flat layer on a plate. Once completely cooled, break the candied pieces apart. In a large bowl, mix all pancake ingredients. Pour about ½ C. batter for each pancake onto a griddle over medium heat and lightly brown each side, turning once. In a large saucepan, combine all ingredients for the Caramel Maple Syrup; cook over medium heat until sugar completely dissolves.

To serve, place pancakes on individual plates and top with syrup and candied pecans.

SWEET POTATO
FRIES
with Chipotle Lime Dip

Chipotle Lime Dip:
1 ¼ C. mayonnaise
Juice from ½ a lime
1 tsp. ground chipotle powder
½ tsp. chili powder
¼ tsp. paprika
¼ tsp. cumin
¼ tsp. garlic powder

Sweet Potato Fries:
4 sweet potatoes or yams
Vegetable oil
Kosher salt

Make the dip by combining all the ingredients in a small bowl. Chill for at least 1 hour before serving so the spices have a chance to blend.

To make the fries, preheat oven to 400 degrees. Cut the sweet potatoes into long sticks and place in a large resealable plastic bag. Add just enough vegetable oil to lightly coat the potatoes; seal the bag and toss to distribute the oil evenly. Layer the potatoes on a cookie sheet. Bake for 35–45 minutes, turning often until lightly browned. Remove from oven and sprinkle with kosher salt to taste. Serve with the Chipotle Lime Dip.

BLUE LEMON'S BUTTERNUT
SQUASH SOUP
Copycat Recipe

SERVES
8

¼ C. butter

¾ C. brown sugar

1 tsp. cinnamon

1 tsp. ginger, freshly grated

1 tsp. nutmeg

½ tsp. cloves

1 ½ C. chicken stock

½ C. apple cider

8 C. butternut squash, cut into 1-inch cubes

2 carrots, sliced

Salt and pepper to taste

1–2 C. heavy cream

Croutons (optional)

Roasted or candied chopped pecans (optional)

In a large pot, melt butter over medium heat. Add brown sugar and spices; stir for 1 minute. Add chicken stock and apple cider. Bring to a boil. Add squash and carrots. Sprinkle with salt and pepper. Cover and simmer for 30 minutes, or until squash and carrots are fork-tender. Check liquid in the pot while simmering and add more chicken stock if necessary. Pour all the contents of the pot into a blender. Puree until mixture is smooth. Blend in 1 C. heavy cream. Gradually add more heavy cream until the mixture reaches the consistency of a creamy soup. Pour the contents of blender back into the pot and keep warm until ready to serve. Garnish soup with croutons and chopped pecans if desired.

SLOW-COOKER
CHICKEN RICE SOUP

SERVES
8

3 chicken breasts, trimmed of fat and cut in half

1 C. parboiled rice, uncooked

1 small onion, chopped

3 carrots, chopped

3 celery stalks, chopped

3 garlic cloves, minced

3 tsp. salt

Pepper to taste

2 tsp. parsley

1 tsp. thyme

½ tsp. rosemary

½ tsp. sage

1 bay leaf

2 T. butter, optional

9 C. chicken broth

Place all ingredients in order in a slow-cooker. Cook on low 3 ½–4 hours. Remove chicken from the slow-cooker and shred or cut into cubes. Return chicken to the slow-cooker and cook for an additional ten minutes before serving.

SHARE YOUR FAVORITE OCTOBER RECIPES WITH YOUR FAMILY AT THE END OF THE SECTION.

On cold autumn nights, what is your favorite soup to make?

SOUP IN A
PUMPKIN

SERVES
8

1 large pumpkin

1 T. butter + ½ C. butter, divided

1 C. white onion, diced

1 ½ C. Italian bread crumbs

1 C. flour

1 T. celery seed

1 lb. Italian sausage, cooked and drained

½ C. Swiss cheese, grated

1 C. cheddar cheese, grated

2 quarts chicken stock or broth

1 tsp. thyme, dried

1 tsp. salt

¼ C. parsley, dried

2 C. fresh kale

1 C. heavy cream

Cut lid off pumpkin. As you are cutting around the stem, angle the knife toward the stem so the ring on the inside of the pulp is smaller than the ring on the outside of the pumpkin. This will make it so the lid won't fall in when it is replaced for baking. Remove seeds. Rub the inside of the lid with 1 T. butter.

Preheat oven to 400. In a skillet, melt ½ C. butter and sauté onions in the melted butter until tender. Add bread crumbs, flour, and celery seed. Stir until coated and cook for 3 minutes. Remove from heat and pour into pumpkin. Add sausage, grated cheeses, chicken stock, thyme, salt, parsley, and kale. Put lid on pumpkin and bake on cookie sheet for 1 ½ hours. Remove from oven. In a medium saucepan, bring cream to a simmer. Add to contents of pumpkin. Stir well. When serving soup, scrape sides of pumpkin with the ladle or a spoon so that bits of pumpkin are added to the soup.

PUMPKIN
ECLAIR CAKE

2 14.4-oz. pkgs. graham crackers
2 3.4-oz. boxes pumpkin spice instant pudding mix
3 ½ C. milk
8 oz. frozen whipped topping, thawed

Frosting:
¾ C. white chocolate chips, melted
2 tsp. light corn syrup
2 tsp. vanilla extract
3 T. butter, softened
1 ½ C. powdered sugar
3 T. milk
Cinnamon to taste (optional)

Cover bottom of a 9 x 13 pan with one layer of whole graham crackers. In a large bowl, combine pudding and milk; beat with a hand mixer for 2 minutes on medium. Gently fold in whipped topping. Pour half of the mixture over the graham crackers and cover with a second layer of graham crackers. Pour remaining pudding mixture over the top and cover with another layer of graham crackers. Refrigerate 2 hours.

Combine frosting ingredients and beat until smooth. Pour over graham crackers and refrigerate overnight. Optional: lightly sprinkle top of cake with cinnamon before serving.

WIZARDING WORLD OF HARRY POTTER
PUMPKIN JUICE

SERVES
16

4 liters apple cider or apple juice
1 15-oz. can pumpkin puree
½ C. sugar
2 tsp. pumpkin pie spice
2 tsp. vanilla

In a large pitcher, combine all ingredients and stir well. Pour over ice in individual glasses.

SHARE YOUR FAVORITE OCTOBER RECIPES WITH YOUR FAMILY AT THE END OF THE SECTION.

What is your favorite pumpkin recipe?

PUMPKIN
STEAMERS

3 C. milk, 2% or whole

1 C. heavy cream

½ C. 100% pure pumpkin puree

½ C. brown sugar

2 T. sweetened condensed milk

2 tsp. pumpkin pie spice

2 tsp. vanilla

Toppings:

Whipped cream

Cinnamon

Place all but topping ingredients in a blender and blend until smooth and frothy. Pour into a large pot and heat on medium high. Stir constantly until warmed through. Pour into mugs; top with whipped cream and sprinkle lightly with cinnamon.

SWEET AND SPICY
PUMPKIN SEEDS

SERVES
8

2 C. pumpkin seeds, rinsed and dried

3 T. butter, melted

1 tsp. salt

¼ tsp. cinnamon

¼ tsp. cumin

¼ tsp. chili powder

¼ tsp. pumpkin pie spice

3 T. brown sugar

1 T. granulated sugar

1 tsp. Worcestershire sauce

2 shakes Tabasco sauce

(more if you like it spicy)

Preheat oven to 300 degrees. In a medium bowl, combine pumpkin seeds and melted butter. Set aside. In a small bowl, combine salt, cinnamon, cumin, chili powder, pumpkin pie spice, brown sugar, and granulated sugar. Sprinkle sugar/spice mixture over seeds and stir well to combine. Add Worcestershire sauce and Tabasco sauce and stir well. Spread pumpkin seeds evenly on a 13 x 18 baking sheet lined with foil or a baking mat. Bake for approximately 45 minutes or until crispy and golden brown.

SHARE YOUR FAVORITE OCTOBER RECIPES WITH YOUR FAMILY AT THE END OF THE SECTION.

Do you have a favorite treat to make on Halloween?

TOFFEE
APPLES

8 small apples (sweet and crisp apples, like Jonagold or Pink Lady, work best)

2 C. sugar

½ C. water

½ tsp. white vinegar

½ tsp. red food coloring

Line a cookie sheet or tray with waxed paper or parchment paper. Wash and dry apples and twist off the stems. Insert a lollipop stick, popsicle stick, or thick wooden skewer into the top of each apple. In a medium-size heavy saucepan, combine sugar, water, and vinegar. Bring the mixture to a boil. To prevent burning on the sides of the pan, use a wet pastry brush to wipe the sugar granules that collect above the boiling mixture. Do not stir the mixture. After mixture is boiling, simmer for 20 minutes, or until it reaches the hard-crack stage (150 C or 295–310 F). Watch it carefully so it doesn't burn. It is best to check often with a candy thermometer. If you don't have a candy thermometer, you can test for the hard-crack stage by dropping a small spoonful of the mixture into a cup of cold water. If it becomes instantly hard (like a piece of hard candy) and cracks when you tap it, it is ready. Remove the pan from the heat. The mixture will be bubbly. It is important to wait until it stops bubbling to dip the apples, or they will be covered with little bubbles. To dip an apple, carefully tip the pan to one side, dip one side of the apple into the mixture, and rotate the apple until it is covered. Allow it to drain a little and place the apple on the waxed paper to cool and harden. Repeat until all apples are coated.

FAVORITE FAMILY RECIPE

SERVES

———

{ RECIPE TITLE }

Ingredients:

Instructions:

FAVORITE FAMILY RECIPE

SERVES

_____

{ RECIPE TITLE }

Ingredients:

_____
_____
_____
_____
_____
_____
_____
_____
_____
_____
_____
_____
_____
_____
_____
_____

Instructions:

_____
_____
_____
_____
_____
_____
_____
_____
_____
_____
_____
_____
_____
_____
_____
_____

CHAPTER 11

NOVEMBER

November

WHAT WE'RE REALLY TALKING ABOUT IS A *wonderful day set aside on the* FOURTH THURSDAY OF NOVEMBER WHEN NO ONE DIETS. *I mean, why else would they call it Thanksgiving?*

—Erma Bombeck, "No One Diets on Thanksgiving," 26 November 1981

November is the month of Thanksgiving, the grand family gathering of the year. We have compiled a list of our favorite recipes for the ultimate Thanksgiving feast: Mom's Famous Roasted Butter Herb Turkey and Turkey Gravy, Perfect Mashed Potatoes, Homemade Crescent Rolls with Herbed Butter, and more. This reminds us of our second favorite quote from Erma Bombeck, one that may remind us a little too much of our family: "I come from a family where gravy is considered a beverage." We love Erma Bombeck!

We do like to stick to many of the traditional favorites for our family Thanksgiving dinner, such as our Mom's version of turkey and turkey gravy. Why mess with perfection? But we'd definitely encourage you to try something new for a side dish or dessert.

We've given you a few here to try. Our Orange Cranberry Sauce has a citrus twist that is incredibly good; it is best served warm over turkey or on a homemade roll. Our Island Pecan Pie became a new favorite several years ago when Emily made it for us. In addition to pecans, it has a creamy base with coconut and pineapple. We never want to have another Thanksgiving dinner without it.

MOM'S FAMOUS ROASTED BUTTER
HERB TURKEY
and Turkey Gravy

SERVES
4

Roasted Butter Herb Turkey:
1 turkey breast or small turkey
½ C. butter
1 T. parsley
1 T. sage
1 T. rosemary
1 T. thyme
½ tsp. salt

Turkey Gravy:
Drippings from turkey
Gravy packet, if included with turkey
1–3 tsp. Wyler's chicken bouillon granules
Pepper to taste
1–2 C. milk
2 T. cornstarch
⅓ C. water

Preheat oven to 325 degrees. Remove any giblets and gravy packets from turkey. Rinse turkey well, inside and out, and pat dry; drying the turkey well will allow the butter to adhere to the turkey. Spray roasting pan or Dutch oven with cooking spray and place turkey in it. Melt butter and brush evenly over turkey. Make slits under the skin layer and brush butter up underneath the skin as well. Combine spices and rub over turkey and under the skin layer. Cover with lid or foil tent and cook according to turkey package directions.

For gravy, leave drippings in roasting pan or Dutch oven. Carefully place on stovetop over medium heat. Remove any pieces of fat from turkey drippings with wire mesh strainer or slotted spoon. If a gravy packet is included with your turkey, add that to the drippings. Whisk up any little browned bits that may have stuck to the roasting pan; these add delicious flavor. Bring to a simmer. Sprinkle in bouillon granules; start with 1 tsp. and add more if needed. Add pepper to taste; stir in milk. Bring back to a simmer. In a separate, small bowl, combine cornstarch and water. Whisking constantly, slowly add cornstarch mixture to simmering gravy until gravy thickens to desired consistency.

HOMEMADE
CRESCENT ROLLS
with Herbed Butter

3 tsp. yeast

2 C. warm water

½ C. butter, softened

⅔ C. nonfat dry milk powder

½ C. sugar

½ C. mashed potato flakes

2 eggs

1 ½ tsp. salt

6 ½ C. flour, divided

Herbed Butter:

½ C. unsalted butter, softened

2 T. fresh parsley, chopped

1 green onion, chopped (white portion only)

1 tsp. fresh thyme leaves, removed from stem

Dash of pepper

In a large bowl, dissolve yeast in warm water. Add butter, dry milk powder, sugar, potato flakes, eggs, salt, and four C. flour. Beat until smooth. Stir in enough remaining flour to form a firm dough ball. Turn onto a heavily floured surface. Knead 8–10 times. Divide into two balls. Roll each ball into a 12-inch circle and cut each circle into 12 wedges. Roll up wedges, starting at widest end, to form a crescent shape. Place rolls on greased cookie sheet. Let rise in a warm place for 1 hour, or until doubled. Bake at 350 degrees for 15–17 minutes, or until golden brown. Serve with herbed butter.

Herbed Butter: In a small bowl, combine all ingredients and mix until well blended. Cover and refrigerate for at least 3 hours before serving. Store in the refrigerator for up to 2 weeks.

COCONUT PECAN
SWEET POTATO

6 medium sweet potatoes or yams, scrubbed and cut in half
¼ C. butter
½ C. sweetened coconut flakes
½ C. pecans, finely chopped
½ C. packed brown sugar

Cinnamon Marshmallow Cream Topping:
1 8-oz. jar marshmallow fluff
1 8-oz. pkg. cream cheese
½ tsp. cinnamon

Preheat oven to 400 degrees. Melt butter; pour onto a cookie sheet and spread evenly over the bottom. Generously sprinkle coconut, pecans, and brown sugar over the butter. Place sweet potato halves facedown on the butter and toppings. Bake for 35–40 minutes until toppings look toasted. Flip sweet potatoes over and generously spoon toppings on top of the sweet potatoes. Bake 15–20 minutes more, or until sweet potatoes are soft. Top with Cinnamon Marshmallow Cream Topping.

Cinnamon Marshmallow Cream Topping: With a hand mixer, blend all ingredients well. Refrigerate until serving. Spoon onto baked sweet potato halves just before eating.

SHARE YOUR FAVORITE NOVEMBER RECIPES WITH YOUR FAMILY AT THE END OF THE SECTION.
What is one of your family's traditional Thanksgiving recipes?

GREEN BEAN
CASSEROLE
with Bacon and Onion Straws

Onion Straws:

1 onion, sliced thin

2 C. buttermilk

1 ½ C. flour

1 tsp. salt

¼ tsp. cayenne pepper

½ tsp. paprika

⅛ tsp. pepper

Oil for frying

Beans and Sauce:

1 lb. fresh green beans, rinsed and trimmed

10 slices bacon

2 T. flour

¾ C. chicken broth

1 C. half-and-half

Pepper to taste

1 C. cheddar cheese, shredded (optional)

To make the onion straws, separate onion rings and place in a large resealable plastic bag. Pour buttermilk over the onions, squeeze the air out of the bag, and refrigerate for at least an hour. In a pie pan or shallow dish, combine flour, salt, cayenne pepper, paprika, and pepper. Heat oil in a skillet or deep pan to 375 degrees. Using tongs, dredge the onion rings in flour mixture, a few at a time, and place in hot oil for 2–3 minutes, or until onions become golden brown. Remove from oil and place on paper towels. Set aside.

To make the beans and sauce, bring a pot of salted water to a boil. Add beans and boil for 5–6 minutes or until beans become tender-crisp. Drain and place in ice water to prevent further cooking. Set aside. In a large skillet over medium-high heat, cook bacon completely. Remove from skillet and drain on paper towels. Set aside. Reduce heat to medium low and drain all but about 2 T. of the bacon grease from the skillet. Sprinkle flour over remaining bacon grease and stir, forming a roux. Whisk in chicken broth and bring to a simmer. Add half-and-half, a little at a time, until sauce thickens to a gravy-like consistency. Add a little milk if needed to thin the sauce. Heat for about 5 minutes, or until sauce barely starts to simmer. Add pepper to taste. Preheat oven to 350 degrees. In a casserole or oven-safe dish, combine beans, sauce, cheese, and half of the bacon. Sprinkle onion straws and remaining bacon over the top and bake for 20 minutes. Serve immediately.

ORANGE
CRANBERRY SAUCE

1 12-oz. bag fresh
cranberries
1 C. orange juice
1 C. sugar
1 tsp. orange zest

In a medium saucepan, combine all ingredients. Bring to a boil, stirring occasionally. The cranberries will soften and begin to pop. Reduce heat and simmer for 10 minutes. Serve warm.

If you want to serve the cranberry sauce chilled, pour sauce into a dish or jar and cool at room temperature. Once cooled, refrigerate until ready to serve.

SHARE YOUR FAVORITE NOVEMBER RECIPES WITH YOUR FAMILY AT THE END OF THE SECTION.

Do you have a favorite
Thanksgiving side recipe?

PERFECT
MASHED POTATOES

4 lbs. russet potatoes

2 tsp. salt

½ C. milk

¼ C. butter

½ C. sour cream

Salt and pepper to taste

Peel potatoes and cut into quarters. Place potatoes in a large stockpot and cover with water. Add salt and bring to a boil. Allow to boil for 20–25 minutes, or until the potatoes fall apart when poked with a fork. In a microwave-safe bowl, combine milk and butter; microwave for about 40 seconds or until butter is melted. This prevents the milk from cooling the potatoes. Drain and mash potatoes, slowly adding the milk/butter mixture, until potatoes reach desired consistency. Mash in sour cream, salt, and pepper. Serve immediately.

Keep potatoes warm until you are ready to serve them by placing them in the oven at 300 degrees in an oven-safe dish covered with tin foil.

THANKSGIVING LEFTOVER
CASSEROLE

2–3 C. leftover turkey, shredded

1 ½ C. cranberry sauce

3–4 C. leftover mashed potatoes

2 C. corn

⅓ C. milk

1–2 C. leftover turkey gravy

4–5 C. leftover stuffing

⅓ C. chicken broth

Preheat oven to 400 degrees. Combine turkey and cranberry sauce and spread evenly on the bottom of a 9 x 13 baking dish. Evenly press leftover mashed potatoes over the turkey, and sprinkle corn over the potatoes. Mix milk and leftover gravy and spread evenly over potatoes and corn. Sprinkle leftover stuffing over the top and drizzle with chicken broth to keep the stuffing from drying out. Cover with tin foil and bake for 35–40 minutes, or until heated through.

BUTTERSCOTCH
PIE

1 ½ C. brown sugar
½ C. flour
1 T. cornstarch
1 tsp. kosher salt
4 C. milk
2 egg yolks
3 T. butter, softened
2 tsp. vanilla
1 precooked pie crust,
homemade or store-bought
Butterscotch topping, store-
bought or homemade
Butterscotch chips
Whipped cream, optional

In a large saucepan, combine the sugar, flour, cornstarch, and salt. Gradually add the milk until it's completely combined and mixture is smooth before putting it over heat. Cook over medium heat until mixture thickens, then remove from heat. In a separate bowl, lightly whisk egg yolks. Add a few spoonfuls of the hot mixture from the stove to the egg yolks and whisk again until smooth. Add the egg yolks to the rest of the hot mixture. Add butter and vanilla. Stir well. Cool in fridge. When ready to eat, pour the mixture into the precooked pie shell. Drizzle with butterscotch topping and sprinkle with butterscotch chips. Top with whipped cream if desired.

ISLAND
PECAN PIE

2 C. sugar

1 T. cornmeal

1 T. flour

5 eggs

Pinch of salt

1 C. pecans, coarsely chopped

1 C. crushed pineapple, thoroughly drained

1 C. flaked coconut

½ C. butter, melted

1 unbaked pie crust

Homemade Almond Whipped Cream:

2 C. heavy cream

3 T. sugar

1 tsp. almond extract

Toasted coconut for garnish

In a large bowl, beat the sugar, cornmeal, flour, eggs, and salt. Gently stir in the pecans, pineapple, and coconut. Stir in the melted butter and mix well. Pour mixture into an unbaked pie crust. Bake at 300 degrees for 50–60 minutes. Remove pie from oven. Cover the crust edge with aluminum foil to keep it from burning. Cook an additional 15–30 minutes, or until the pie is set. Allow pie to cool at room temperature, then refrigerate until ready to serve. Top with Homemade Almond Whipped Cream.

Homemade Almond Whipped Cream: With a mixer, whip heavy cream until soft peaks form. Add sugar and almond extract. Continue to whip until stiff peaks form or until it reaches desired consistency. Top with toasted coconut.

SHARE YOUR FAVORITE NOVEMBER RECIPES WITH YOUR FAMILY AT THE END OF THE SECTION.

What is your favorite pie recipe?

TRADITIONAL
PUMPKIN PIE

Crust:

1 ¾ C. flour

2 tsp. sugar

1 tsp. salt

⅓ C. unsalted butter

⅓ C. shortening

7–8 T. cold water

Pumpkin Filling:

2 eggs

¾ C. sugar

1 tsp. cinnamon

½ tsp. ginger

½ tsp. nutmeg

½ tsp. salt

¼ tsp. cloves

1 15-oz. can pumpkin

1 12-oz. can evaporated milk

Whipped Topping:

1 pint whipping cream

¼ C. sugar

2 tsp. almond or amaretto flavoring

To make the crust: In a large bowl, combine flour, sugar, and salt. Add the butter and shortening; mix with a pastry blender until blended and crumbly. Slowly add cold water while stirring with a fork just until blended; do not overmix. Form dough into a ball, wrap in plastic wrap, and cool in the refrigerator for at least 30 minutes. Place dough on a lightly floured surface and roll out into a large circle. Fold the dough in half so it is easy to transfer to a 9-inch pie pan; unfold over pan. Shape dough into pan and pinch along the top edge to create the crust design. Leave unbaked.

To make the filling: In a large bowl, whisk eggs until blended. Stir in sugar and spices. Mix in the pumpkin. Gradually stir in the evaporated milk. Pour into the unbaked pie crust and bake for 15 minutes at 425 degrees. Turn the oven down to 350 degrees and bake 40–50 minutes or until a knife in the center comes out clean. Remove from oven and cool completely before cutting.

To make the whipped topping: Beat all ingredients until stiff peaks form. Spoon onto cooled pie and sprinkle with cinnamon.

FAVORITE FAMILY RECIPE

SERVES

_____

{ RECIPE TITLE }

Ingredients:

_____
_____
_____
_____
_____
_____
_____
_____
_____
_____
_____
_____
_____
_____
_____
_____
_____
_____

Instructions:

_____
_____
_____
_____
_____
_____
_____
_____
_____
_____
_____
_____
_____
_____
_____
_____
_____
_____
_____
_____
_____

FAVORITE FAMILY RECIPE

SERVES

_____

{ RECIPE TITLE }

Ingredients:

_____
_____
_____
_____
_____
_____
_____
_____
_____
_____
_____
_____
_____
_____
_____
_____
_____
_____
_____
_____

Instructions:

_____
_____
_____
_____
_____
_____
_____
_____
_____
_____
_____
_____
_____
_____
_____
_____
_____
_____
_____

CHAPTER 12

DECEMBER

December

WINTER IS THE TIME FOR COMFORT,

For good food and warmth,

FOR THE TOUCH OF A FRIENDLY HAND

and for a talk beside the fire;

IT IS THE TIME FOR HOME.

—Edith Sitwell

December is the most delightful time of year to spend time cooking in the kitchen. We turn on our favorite Christmas music, fill a mug with cocoa, and hope Mother Nature will do her part with some gently falling snow just outside the kitchen window while we are preparing some Old-Fashioned Chocolate-Covered Cherries or our copycat version of See's Fudge.

Food can create so many beautiful memories during the holidays. Gathering friends for a cookie exchange, meeting with coworkers for a Christmas dinner, or helping with a Christmas party at church or school are all occasions that are made even better by preparing something extra special. Our Christmas Salad with Creamy Poppy Seed Dressing is a light and colorful salad that complements the rich meats and creamy side dishes at a Christmas dinner. Our Cranberry Almond Bacon Cheese Ball is a flavorful appetizer for a dinner or party. Candy Cane Hot Chocolate makes regular hot chocolate extra festive.

Planning ahead is the key to enjoyable December cooking and baking. Early in the month, make a list of the appetizers, main dishes, and desserts you know you want to make so you can have the ingredients on hand for cooking and baking days. Extra trips to the grocery store can be very time-consuming and frustrating! Be sure to ask your family about their favorite recipes and recruit their help with the preparations.

CANDY CANE
HOT CHOCOLATE

SERVES
8-10

1 C. whipping cream
1 14-oz. can sweetened condensed milk
8 C. milk
1 tsp. peppermint extract
2 C. white chocolate chips
Whipped topping
Crushed candy canes

Combine the cream, milks, peppermint extract, and chocolate chips in a slow-cooker or in a large pot over low heat. Stir occasionally until chocolate chips have melted. Bring to desired temperature. Serve in mugs and top with whipped topping and crushed candy cane pieces.

CHRISTMAS
QUICHE

1 9-inch unbaked pie crust, frozen or homemade

½ lb. ground sausage

¾ C. dried cranberries

3 eggs, lightly beaten

1 ½ C. half-and-half

1 ½ C. Monterey Jack cheese, shredded

Preheat oven to 400 degrees. Bake pie shell for 7 minutes. If using a frozen pie shell, let it sit 10 minutes at room temperature before baking. Let cool. Reduce oven temperature to 375 degrees. Brown sausage; drain excess grease. Stir in dried cranberries. In a medium bowl, whisk eggs and half-and-half until well blended. Sprinkle cheese on the bottom of the pie shell. Cover with sausage and cranberries. Pour egg mixture into pie shell over sausage, cranberries, and cheese. Bake 45 minutes or until knife inserted into center comes out clean. Let stand 10 minutes before serving.

SHARE YOUR FAVORITE DECEMBER RECIPES WITH YOUR FAMILY AT THE END OF THE SECTION.

Do you have a special breakfast recipe for Christmas morning?

EGGNOG
FRENCH TOAST
with Gingerbread Syrup

SERVES
8

Eggnog French Toast:
1 loaf French bread
2 ½ C. eggnog
6 eggs
½ C. brown sugar
1 tsp. cinnamon
½ tsp. salt
½ tsp. nutmeg
1 tsp. vanilla
Cinnamon and sugar for topping

Gingerbread Syrup:
2 C. water
1 C. brown sugar
½ C. Biscoff spread
½ C. white corn syrup
¼ tsp. ginger
¼ tsp. cinnamon
¼ tsp. nutmeg
Whipped topping (optional)

To make Eggnog French Toast: Cut bread into thick slices and arrange in a 9 x 13 baking pan lightly sprayed with nonstick cooking spray. In a large bowl, beat eggnog, eggs, brown sugar, spices, and vanilla. Pour mixture over bread slices; turn the slices of bread a few times to ensure good coating. Sprinkle the tops with a little cinnamon and sugar. Cover and refrigerate overnight or for at least 3 hours. In the morning, bake for 45 minutes at 350 degrees, or until golden brown. Serve with Gingerbread Syrup and whipped topping if desired.

To make Gingerbread Syrup: In a small saucepan, combine all syrup ingredients over medium-high heat. Bring to a low boil, then remove from heat. Serve over French toast.

CRANBERRY ALMOND BACON
CHEESE BALL

SERVES
6

8 oz. cream cheese, softened
8 oz. white cheddar (you can also use feta, goat cheese, or Gorgonzola)
½ C. bacon, cooked and crumbled
½ C. dried cranberries (Craisins work great!)
1 T. cilantro, finely chopped
1 tsp. Worcestershire sauce
½ C. roasted almonds, chopped

In a medium bowl, whip softened cream cheese until it is creamy and has no lumps. Stir in white cheddar, bacon, cranberries, cilantro, and Worcestershire sauce and mix well. Spoon mixture onto a large piece of plastic wrap. Bring corners together and form mixture into a large ball. Place in a bowl and refrigerate for at least 3 hours, or until cheese ball becomes firm. Once the cheese ball has set up, roll it in the chopped almonds until completely coated. Serve with sliced baguette bread or crackers.

CHRISTMAS
SALAD

Salad:

6 C. spring mix lettuce

½ C. mandarin oranges

⅓ C. dried cranberries

⅓ C. pomegranate seeds

⅓ C. Feta cheese

½ C. candied walnuts or pecans

Creamy Poppy Seed Dressing:

⅓ C. mayonnaise

⅓ C. Greek yogurt

4 T. sugar

2 T. apple cider vinegar

2 tsp. poppy seeds

In a large bowl, top lettuce with remaining salad ingredients.

To make the Creamy Poppy Seed Dressing: In a small bowl, combine all ingredients and whisk until smooth. Keep refrigerated until serving.

SHARE YOUR FAVORITE DECEMBER RECIPES WITH YOUR FAMILY AT THE END OF THE SECTION.

Do you have a traditional Christmas Eve or Christmas Day dinner recipe?

SLOW-COOKER MOLTEN CHOCOLATE
CARAMEL CAKE

Parchment paper
1 box devil's food cake mix,
unprepared
1 ¼ C. milk
½ C. vegetable oil
3 eggs
1 3.9-oz. instant chocolate
pudding mix
2 C. milk

For the top layer:
1 bag Rolo mini candies,
unwrapped

Cut out a large piece of parchment paper and place it in a slow-cooker on low heat; you can also use a slow-cooker liner. Lightly spray with cooking spray. In a large bowl, mix the cake mix, milk, oil, and eggs. Beat for 2 minutes. Pour over the parchment paper in the slow-cooker. In a medium bowl, mix the instant pudding mix and milk; beat for 2 minutes. Carefully and evenly pour the pudding over the cake layer in the slow-cooker; do not mix it in! Carefully arrange a layer of Rolo mini candies over the top of pudding layer but do not mix in. Place lid on slow-cooker and cook on low for 3 hours or until a toothpick inserted in the center comes out clean. It will become a layer of chocolate cake over a gooey, chocolate caramel sauce. Spoon into individual bowls and serve warm with vanilla ice cream.

OLD-FASHIONED CHOCOLATE-COVERED
CHERRIES

SERVES
60

60 maraschino cherries, with or without stems

3 T. butter, softened

3 T. corn syrup

2 C. powdered sugar

1–1½ lbs. real milk chocolate or semisweet chocolate melts (the better the quality chocolate, the better they taste)

Drain cherries and set on paper towel until dry. In a medium bowl, combine butter and corn syrup until smooth. Stir in powdered sugar and knead to form a dough. Chill to stiffen if necessary. Wrap each cherry in about 1 tsp. of dough. Chill until firm. In a microwave-safe bowl, melt chocolate 30 seconds at a time. Stir after each 30 seconds until chocolate is just melted and completely smooth. Dip each cherry in chocolate and place on waxed-paper-lined cookie sheet. Let cool at room temperature. Place in an airtight container and store in a cool place for 2 weeks (yes, it is a long time, but they taste best if you wait!).

SHARE YOUR FAVORITE DECEMBER RECIPES WITH YOUR FAMILY AT THE END OF THE SECTION.

What are your favorite family Christmas treats?

ABOUT
48
SQUARES

SEE'S
FUDGE
Copycat Recipe

16 oz. milk chocolate (2 8-ounce Hershey bars broken into pieces work great)

24 oz. semisweet chocolate chips

½ C. butter

1 7-oz. jar marshmallow whip

4 ¼ C. sugar

12 oz. evaporated milk

In a large mixing bowl, combine chocolate bars, chocolate chips, butter, and marshmallow whip. Set aside. In a large saucepan, combine sugar and evaporated milk. Bring to a rolling boil over medium heat. Stir constantly for 4 minutes. Pour cooked ingredients over chocolate in mixing bowl in 4–6 intervals, stirring constantly until smooth. Pour into a buttered 9 x 13 glass baking dish. Cover tightly and refrigerate until set. Keep refrigerated.

CREAMY ONE-POT
TORTELLINI

1 T. oil

1 lb. smoked sausage, sliced

3 cloves garlic, minced

2–3 C. broccoli florets

5 oz. frozen tortellini

1 15-oz. can petite diced tomatoes, undrained

1 8-oz. can tomato sauce

½ C. chicken broth

½ T. basil

1 tsp. oregano

⅓ C. Parmesan cheese

4 oz. cream cheese

Salt and pepper to taste

In a large skillet over medium-high heat, heat oil. Add sausage and sauté until brown and slightly crispy on each side. Add garlic and sauté another minute. Add broccoli, tortellini, diced tomatoes, tomato sauce, chicken broth, basil, and oregano. Bring to a boil, cover, and simmer for 7–8 minutes, or until broccoli is cooked. Add Parmesan cheese, cream cheese, salt, and pepper to taste. Stir until cheese melts. Heat on low for another 3–5 minutes. Serve immediately.

THE BEST
CLAM CHOWDER

¾ C. butter, melted

1 C. flour

1 C. celery, finely diced

1 C. onions, finely diced

1 C. leeks, finely diced

3 C. red potatoes, diced (use less for a thinner chowder)

¾ C. clams, shelled and chopped

¾ T. fresh ground pepper

1 ½ T. kosher salt

¾ T. whole thyme

6 bay leaves

4 shakes Tabasco sauce

3 C. chicken broth

¾ C. clam juice

2 quarts half-and-half

In a glass baking dish, combine melted butter and flour; bake at 325 degrees for 25–30 minutes, or until golden brown and crumbly. In a large skillet, soften celery, onion, and leeks in a little butter or oil for 3–5 minutes, or until soft and slightly transparent. Remove from heat and place in a large pot with remaining ingredients except the half-and-half and butter-flour mixture. Bring to a boil, then reduce heat and simmer for about 10 minutes or until potatoes are cooked through and no longer crunchy in the middle. Stir butter-flour mixture into the chowder until thick. Mixture will be slightly less thick than cookie dough. Remove chowder from heat and stir in half-and-half until blended and smooth. Heat to serving temperature (do not bring to a boil), stirring occasionally. It should be creamy and smooth. Add salt and pepper for extra flavor.

FAVORITE FAMILY RECIPE

SERVES

—

{ RECIPE TITLE }

Ingredients:

Instructions:

FAVORITE FAMILY RECIPE

SERVES

{ RECIPE TITLE }

Ingredients:

Instructions:

12 days of
CHRISTMAS TREATS

Christmas Treats

WE ELVES TRY TO STICK TO

the four main food groups:

CANDY, CANDY CANES,

Candy Corns, and Syrup.

—Buddy the Elf

A favorite Christmas tradition in our home growing up was preparing and delivering Christmas treats to our friends and neighbors. We have wonderful memories of baking cookies, making fudge, and wrapping homemade caramels. We spread bright-red paper plates on the table and loaded them with all of the goodies. We wrapped them in cellophane and topped them with a big Christmas bow. It was usually late afternoon or evening by the time we were finished. We bundled up in our coats, hats, mittens, and boots and set off into the cold night air with our gifts. It was so much fun to take those plates around, visit with our neighbors, and wish them a Merry Christmas.

These recipes for Twelve Days of Christmas Treats are easy to make as gifts for friends, coworkers, teachers, and neighbors during the holidays—and also for your own family to enjoy!

hot chocolate mix

Add three heaping
spoonfuls of hot
chocolate mix to a
mug of hot water.

HOT
CHOCOLATE MIX

SERVES
45

4 C. powdered dry milk

4 C. chocolate drink mix
(Nestle Nesquik)

2 C. powdered sugar

1 ½ C. powdered coffee
creamer

In a large bowl, mix all ingredients until well blended. Store mix in a sealed container. To serve, mix 4 heaping spoonfuls of mix into 6–8 ounces hot water.

SHARE YOUR FAVORITE CHRISTMAS GIFT RECIPES WITH YOUR FAMILY AT THE END OF THE SECTION.

*Do you have a favorite
Christmas food gift recipe?*

CHOCOLATE
ORANGE COOKIES

¾ C. packed brown sugar

¾ C. granulated sugar

1 C. Country Crock butter spread

1 large egg

1 large egg yolk

2 tsp. vanilla extract

3 C. all-purpose flour

1 tsp. baking powder

¾ tsp. salt

¾ tsp. baking soda

⅓ C. cocoa powder

1 milk or dark chocolate orange, chopped

⅓ C. mini chocolate chips

2 tsp. orange zest

Preheat oven to 375 degrees. In a large bowl, mix brown sugar, granulated sugar, Country Crock spread, egg, egg yolk, and vanilla. Stir in flour, baking powder, salt, baking soda, and cocoa powder until blended. Add chopped chocolate orange, mini chocolate chips, and orange zest. Mix until well combined. Drop dough by rounded tablespoons onto ungreased baking sheets 3 inches apart. Bake 10–12 minutes, or until edges are lightly golden. Cool 1 minute on wire rack. Remove from baking sheets and cool completely.

CHRISTMAS CRUNCH
POPCORN SNACK

SERVES
8-10

2 bags gourmet white microwave popcorn, popped and kernels removed

3 C. mini pretzels

1 large bag red and green M&Ms

2 C. peanuts, roasted and salted

18 oz. white candy melts

Red and green sprinkles

In a large bowl, combine popcorn, pretzels, M&Ms, and peanuts. In a microwave-safe bowl, microwave white candy melts in 30-second intervals, stirring the chocolate until melted and smooth. Drizzle over the popcorn mix and stir until coated. Add sprinkles and toss until evenly distributed. Spread over waxed paper and let cool. Store in an airtight container until ready to serve.

SLOW-COOKER CINNAMON
ALMONDS

1 ¼ C. sugar

1 ¼ C. brown sugar

2 T. cinnamon

½ tsp. salt

1 egg white

2 tsp. vanilla

3 C. plain raw almonds

¼ C. water

Preheat slow-cooker on low. In a large bowl, mix sugars, cinnamon, and salt. In a separate bowl, beat egg white and vanilla with a hand mixer until frothy. Put almonds in a large resealable plastic bag. Pour in the egg mixture. Seal and toss, making sure the almonds are thoroughly coated so the cinnamon/sugar mix will stick to the almonds during the cooking process. Spray slow-cooker with cooking spray. Put the almonds from the plastic bag into the slow-cooker. Pour the cinnamon-sugar mix over the almonds and stir until coated. Cook on low for 3 hours, stirring every 20–30 minutes.

The mix around the almonds will be dry until the last step. When the almonds have cooked the desired amount of time, add ¼ C. water to the slow-cooker and stir well. This will ensure a crunchy coating and help the sugars stick to the almonds and harden. Line a baking sheet with parchment paper and spread the almonds onto the sheet to cool. The almonds should be sticky, so be sure to separate them the best you can. Allow almonds to cool completely.

SLOW-COOKER
PEANUT CLUSTERS

1 12-oz. bag white chocolate chips
1 12-oz. bag semisweet chocolate chips
1 lb. white chocolate almond bark
2 lbs. peanuts, lightly salted

Combine all ingredients in a large slow-cooker; cook on low for 1 hour, stirring once after 30 minutes. Using a spoon, scoop clumps of peanut mixture onto waxed paper and allow to cool to room temperature. If you want to make a decorative topping, melt some white chocolate chips or vanilla melts and drizzle over the top.

DIPPED RITZ
COOKIES

Caramel Cookies:
13.7 oz. Ritz crackers
12 oz. Rolo caramel candies
Chocolate chips or baking chocolate bars
Sprinkles (optional)

Peanut Butter Cookies:
1 C. peanut butter
½ C. powdered sugar
13.7 oz. Ritz crackers
White chocolate chips or baking white chocolate bars
Sprinkles (optional)

To make Caramel Cookies: Lay half of the crackers (about 50–60) face down on a cookie sheet. Top each cracker with one Rolo candy. Bake at 300 degrees for about 5 minutes. Remove from oven and quickly top each softened Rolo candy with another cracker. Press down on the crackers a little, but not so much that the caramel comes out the sides. Cool completely. Melt chocolate chips or chocolate bars; dip cooled cookies in chocolate. Place on parchment paper to cool. If adding sprinkles, be sure to do so before the chocolate sets. Chocolate should set up and become firm before cookies are eaten.

To make Peanut Butter Cookies: In a small bowl, mix peanut butter and powdered sugar. Top each cracker with a little heap of peanut butter. Press down on each cracker a little, but not so much that the peanut butter comes out the sides. Melt the chocolate chips or chocolate bars; dip the cookies in chocolate. Place on parchment paper to cool. If adding sprinkles, be sure to do so before the chocolate sets. Chocolate should set up and become firm before cookies are eaten.

Tips on dipping: Melt a small amount of chocolate at a time. Fill a small 8-oz. glass bowl with chocolate and heat in the microwave in 30-second increments until melted, stirring after each interval. Use a plastic fork with the middle prongs broken off to dip the cookie into the chocolate. Pick up the cookie with the fork and gently tap it against the side of the bowl to let the excess chocolate drip off.

ENGLISH TOFFEE

¼ tsp. salt
½ tsp. vanilla
1 C. butter
1 C. sugar
½ C. semisweet chocolate chips
Nuts (optional)

In a saucepan, combine all ingredients; stir over medium heat until butter and sugar are dissolved, then bring to a rolling boil. Boil until mixture turns a caramel brown and reaches the hard-crack stage, around 310 degrees. Spread a handful of your favorite nuts on a cookie sheet sprayed with nonstick cooking spray. Pour the hot toffee over the nuts and spread flat. Immediately sprinkle a handful of chocolate chips over toffee. When the chocolate chips start to melt, spread them evenly over the toffee. When chocolate sets, break the toffee into pieces. Store in an airtight container.

GERMAN CHOCOLATE
FUDGE

Fudge:

1 C. butter, cut into slices

2 C. semisweet chocolate chips

2 C. milk chocolate chips

4 ½ C. sugar

12 oz. evaporated milk

1 tsp. vanilla

German Chocolate Frosting:

1 C. sugar

1 C. evaporated milk

½ C. butter

3 egg yolks

1 tsp. vanilla

1 ½ C. flaked coconut

1 C. chopped pecans

To make the fudge: In a large bowl of mixer, combine butter slices and chocolate chips. Use butter wrapper to grease bottom of a 9 x 13 pan. In a 2-quart or larger saucepan, bring sugar and milk to a boil, stirring constantly; be careful not to scorch. Boil 10 minutes, stirring constantly. Remove from heat and pour into bowl with the butter and chocolate chips. Beat for 3 minutes with mixer. Add vanilla and mix thoroughly. Spread warm fudge into the buttered 9 x 13 pan. Let cool completely before adding topping.

To make the frosting: In a large saucepan, combine sugar, milk, butter, and egg yolks before setting pan on the stove. Bring mix to a boil over medium heat until it thickens, 6–8 minutes. Remove from heat and add vanilla, coconut, and pecans. Let mixture cool completely before spreading on fudge. Store in refrigerator in an airtight container.

SHARE YOUR FAVORITE CHRISTMAS GIFT RECIPES WITH YOUR FAMILY AT THE END OF THE SECTION.

What is your favorite fudge recipe?

GINGERBREAD
COOKIES

¾ C. butter, softened

1 C. brown sugar

1 egg

¾ C. molasses

4 C. flour

2 tsp. ground ginger

1 ½ tsp. baking soda

1 ½ tsp. ground cinnamon

¾ tsp. ground cloves

¼ tsp. salt

White frosting (royal icing works well)

Small candies, chocolate chips, or raisins for decorating

In a large bowl, cream butter and sugar until smooth. Add egg and molasses. Set aside. In a separate bowl, mix all dry ingredients. Slowly add dry ingredients to wet ingredients, stirring constantly. Mix until combined. Cover and refrigerate for at least 4 hours. Remove from fridge and bring to room temperature. Preheat oven to 350 degrees. On a floured surface, roll dough out to about ⅛-inch thickness. Cut with cookie cutters and place on a greased baking sheet. Bake for 8–10 minutes. Decorate with icing and candy if desired.

PEANUT
DIVINITY

4 C. sugar

1 C. light corn syrup

1 C. cold water

3 egg whites

1 tsp. vanilla

1 C. roasted peanuts

Topping:

½ C. mini chocolate chips, melted

Chopped roasted peanuts

In a saucepan over medium-high heat, mix sugar, corn syrup, and water. Stir until sugar has dissolved, then add the candy thermometer and stop stirring. Watch for the candy thermometer to reach exactly 255 degrees; immediately remove from heat. While the sugar is heating, use a stand mixer with a large bowl to beat the egg whites. Beat until the egg whites are bright white, fluffy, and form stiff peaks. When the sugar mixture reaches 255 degrees, slowly pour it onto the egg whites while the mixer is running at a fast speed. Drizzle the hot mixture into the egg whites very slowly; it should take up to 5 minutes to pour it all in. After you have poured in all the hot mixture, continue to beat at a high speed for 8–10 minutes. Beat in vanilla and stir in peanuts. Using two spoons, drop dollops of divinity onto waxed or parchment paper. Move quickly—the divinity will start to stiffen. Let cool completely; drizzle with melted chocolate chips and sprinkle with chopped peanuts.

Pecan Chewies

1 Jar Pecan Chewie mix
1/2 cup butter

1 egg
1 tsp vanilla extract

Preheat oven to 350. Cream the butter, egg and vanilla together until smooth. Add the Pecan Chewie Mix and stir until combined. Drop onto greased cookie sheet. Bake for 10 to 12 minutes.

PECAN CHEWIE

Mix in a Jar

½ C. butter

½ C. sugar

½ C. firmly packed brown sugar

1 egg

1 tsp. vanilla

¾ C. flour

½ tsp. baking soda

½ tsp. baking powder

1 ¼ C. old-fashioned oats

¾ C. chopped pecans

1 C. Rice Krispies cereal

Preheat oven to 350 degrees. In a large bowl, cream butter, sugar, and brown sugar. Mix in egg and vanilla. In a separate bowl, whisk flour, baking soda, and baking powder. Stir in oats, pecans, and rice cereal. Mix dry ingredients into wet ingredients. Scoop dough in approximately 1½-inch balls onto a greased cookie sheet. Bake for 10–12 minutes.

To make Pecan Chewie Mix in a Jar: Using a wide-mouth, quart-size glass jar, layer ingredients. Start with white sugar on the bottom and end with the flour mixed with 1/2 tsp. baking soda and 1/2 tsp. baking powder. After you add each ingredient, press it down firmly in the jar using the bottom of a narrow drinking glass or cup. Place the lid on the jar and tie a copy of the instructions onto the jar with a decorative ribbon.

SHARE YOUR FAVORITE CHRISTMAS GIFT RECIPES WITH YOUR FAMILY AT THE END OF THE SECTION.

What is your favorite Christmas cookie recipe?

WHITE CHOCOLATE PEPPERMINT
BARK BROWNIES

2 boxes brownie mix

Sour cream

1 8-oz. pkg. cream cheese, softened

¼ C. butter, softened

½ tsp. vanilla

½ tsp. almond extract

1 C. white chocolate chips or bark

2 C. powdered sugar

Candy canes, crushed into small pieces

Prepare brownie mixes according to package directions with one exception: use half water and half sour cream (for example, if the brownie mix calls for ½ C. water, use ¼ C. water and ¼ C. sour cream instead). Pour into a 13 x 18 cookie sheet sprayed with nonstick cooking spray. Bake at 325 degrees for 25–30 minutes, or until a toothpick a few inches from the edge comes out mostly clean. Cool completely before frosting.

To make the frosting, beat cream cheese and butter. Add vanilla and almond extract. Melt the white chocolate, then slowly blend it in. Add powdered sugar and mix until thoroughly blended. Spread over cooled brownies. Sprinkle candy cane pieces over the frosting.

FAVORITE FAMILY RECIPE

SERVES

{ RECIPE TITLE }

Ingredients:

Instructions:

FAVORITE FAMILY RECIPE

SERVES

_____

{ RECIPE TITLE }

Ingredients:

_____
_____
_____
_____
_____
_____
_____
_____
_____
_____
_____
_____
_____
_____
_____
_____

Instructions:

_____
_____
_____
_____
_____
_____
_____
_____
_____
_____
_____
_____
_____
_____
_____
_____
_____
_____
_____
_____
_____
_____
_____

CHAPTER 13

Cooking for a

CROWD

Cooking for a Crowd

THE MOST INDISPENSABLE

ingredient of all

GOOD HOME COOKING:

love for those you are cooking for.

—Sophia Loren

Times have come for all four of us when we have needed to figure out recipes to feed large groups of people. There are family reunions as well as church, school, and work events. There are bridal showers, baby showers, and book clubs. Family and friends come to visit. All of our recipes can be doubled, tripled, and multiplied to fit the needs of a larger group—but that isn't always possible to do in a single-home kitchen. In this section we've put together four menu-plan ideas that work well when cooking for a crowd.

Breakfast or Brunch for a Crowd of Two Dozen

If you are hosting a breakfast of brunch for a crowd, here are two great recipes that can be used separately or together. Our Slow-Cooker Breakfast Casserole and Cake Mix Coffee Cake can be served together or separately with a fresh fruit tray, fruit juice, and/or milk for a delicious start to the day. Both recipes serve 24.

SLOW-COOKER BREAKFAST
CASSEROLE

SERVES
24

---

24 breakfast sausage links

24 eggs

2 C. milk

Salt and pepper to taste

4 lbs. Potatoes O'Brien (hash-browns with diced onions and peppers)

2 tomatoes, diced

4 C. cheddar cheese, shredded

Sour cream for topping (optional)

Salsa for topping (optional)

(You will need two slow-cookers for this recipe)

Brown sausage links in skillet until cooked through; cut into pieces. Set aside. In a very large bowl, beat eggs and milk. Add salt and pepper. Stir in cut-up sausage, Potatoes O'Brien, tomatoes, and cheese. Spray two slow-cookers with nonstick cooking spray and divide egg mixture between the two. Cook on low for 6–7 hours.

If desired, top servings with sour cream and/or salsa.

SERVES
24

CAKE MIX
COFFEE CAKE

Cakes:
2 15- to 18-oz. yellow cake mixes, unprepared
1 C. water
1 C. buttermilk
⅔ C. oil (coconut oil works great)
6 eggs
2 3.4-oz. pkgs. vanilla instant pudding mix
2 C. sour cream

Topping:
2 C. brown sugar
½ C. granulated sugar
2 C. flour
4 tsp. cinnamon
1 tsp. kosher salt
1 C. butter
2 C. walnuts or pecans, chopped (optional)

(You will need two 9x13 pans for this recipe)

Preheat oven to 350 degrees. In an extra-large bowl, combine cake mixes, water, buttermilk, oil, eggs, and pudding mixes. Beat with a mixer for about 2 minutes. Fold in sour cream. Pour batter evenly between two greased 9 x 13 glass baking dishes. In a smaller bowl, combine sugars, flour, cinnamon, and salt. Cut butter into small pieces and add to the sugar mixture. Mix together with a fork or pastry blender until crumbly. Stir in walnuts or pecans. Divide half of the topping and sprinkle over the batter in each pan (put ¼ of the topping on one cake and ¼ of the topping on the other cake). Use a knife to swirl the mixture throughout the cakes. Top each cake evenly with remaining topping. (If desired, you can also put all of the topping on the top of the cakes, as shown in the picture.) Bake 35–45 minutes or until a toothpick inserted into the center comes out clean.

Baking tip: If both 9 x 13 pans fit in your oven side by side, switch the pans halfway through the baking time so both cakes cook more evenly. If the two pans do not fit in your oven side by side, place one on the top rack and one on the bottom rack; switch the pans halfway through the baking time.

324 COOKING FOR A CROWD

SHARE YOUR FAVORITE CROWD RECIPES WITH
YOUR FAMILY AT THE END OF THE SECTION.

*What is your go-to recipe when cooking
breakfast for a crowd?*

Lunch or Picnic for a Crowd of Two Dozen

If you are hosting a crowd for a lunch (or a light dinner), or if you're providing a picnic lunch at a park, these recipes are great because they can be made ahead of time and are easy to transport. The Turkey over Italy French Bread Sandwiches are made on a large loaf of French bread; when ready to serve, they are sliced into individual portions. Our Summer Pasta Salad is festive and colorful and is the perfect side for the sandwich. You can easily add some fruit, carrot and celery sticks, or bags of chips to offer some variety. Our Picnic Cake is the ideal dessert to finish off the lunch. It isn't frosted, which makes it easy to eat, serve, and transport, if necessary.

TURKEY OVER ITALY FRENCH BREAD
SANDWICHES

SERVES
20-24

4 loaves French bread

2 C. mayonnaise

1 C. pesto

2 lbs. sliced provolone cheese

4 lbs. deli turkey

8 C. shredded lettuce

4 T. red wine vinegar

2 tsp. oregano

2 C. sliced pepperoncini

Slice the French bread loaves in half horizontally and lay the halves flat. Combine mayonnaise and pesto and stir until well combined; spread evenly over the bread. Layer ½ lb. cheese and 1 lb. turkey over each sandwich. Toss shredded lettuce with red wine vinegar and oregano and place evenly over each sandwich. Top each sandwich with ½ C. pepperoncini and place "top" on each sandwich. Cut each loaf into 5–6 sections and serve.

SUMMER
PASTA SALAD

2 16-oz. pkgs. tri-colored spiral pasta

2 16-oz. bottles Italian or Zesty Italian salad dressing

2 C. quartered artichoke hearts

2 C. cherry tomatoes, halved

1 6.5-oz. can olives, sliced

2 green, yellow, or red bell peppers, chopped

12 sticks string cheese, sliced into rounds

2 14-oz. cans chopped baby corn

2 avocados, diced

Other topping options:
Chopped pepperoni
Chopped broccoli
Sun-dried tomatoes
Chopped grilled chicken
Chopped onions
Parmesan cheese

Cook pasta according to package directions. Drain pasta well and rinse with cold water until completely cooled. Toss pasta with all ingredients except avocado. Add dressing. Cover and refrigerate at least 4 hours before serving. Add avocado just before serving.

PICNIC
CAKE

1 C. butter

2 C. quick-cooking oatmeal

3 ½ C. boiling water

2 C. brown sugar

2 C. white sugar

4 eggs

3 ½ C. flour

2 tsp. baking soda

2 T. cocoa

1 tsp. salt

2 tsp. cinnamon

24 oz. chocolate chips, divided

Chopped pecan or walnut pieces (optional)

(You will need 2 9x13 pans for this recipe)

In an extra-large bowl, combine butter and oatmeal; pour boiling water over butter and oatmeal. Let sit 10 minutes until butter is melted. Add sugars and mix well with a spoon. Add eggs and mix well. Stir in dry ingredients and half the chocolate chips. Divide batter evenly between two greased and floured 9 x 13 pans. Sprinkle remaining chocolate chips and nuts on top. Bake 30–35 minutes at 350 degrees. This cake is delicious on its own but is also good topped with whipped cream or vanilla ice cream.

Baking tip: If both 9 x 13 pans fit in your oven side by side, switch the pans halfway through the baking time so both cakes cook more evenly. If the two pans will not fit in your oven side by side, place one on the top rack and one on the bottom rack. Switch the pans halfway through the baking time.

SHARE YOUR FAVORITE CROWD RECIPES WITH YOUR FAMILY AT THE END OF THE SECTION.

Do you have a favorite dessert recipe that serves more than 20?

Chili and Cornbread
Dinner for Fifty

This is a casual dinner or lunch menu for a very large crowd. If you are hosting a large group, we hope you have some extra helpers! Like our other meals for a crowd, much of this meal can be prepared ahead of time. This is an easy chili recipe with a short list of ingredients that can be purchased in bulk. The chili is a hearty meal on its own, especially when served with the cornbread or cornbread muffins. For some variation, it can also be served with tortilla chips, sour cream, and shredded cheese. Another option is to serve it over baked potatoes with shredded cheese and sour cream for a satisfying and filling meal. We have included a Chocolate Chip Pumpkin Sheet Cake dessert recipe as an optional dessert.

SERVES
50-60

MOM'S
CHEATER CHILI

5 lbs. ground beef

5 onions, diced

1 6-lb. can chili (any brand)

1 6-lb. can chili beans, undrained

1 6-lb. can diced tomatoes

1 quart (46 oz.) tomato juice

Salt and pepper to taste

Optional Toppings:
Shredded cheese
Diced onions
Sour cream

In a very large, high-walled skillet, brown ground beef. Drain excess liquid and add onion. Cook until onion becomes soft and transparent. Put meat/onion mixture and remaining ingredients in a large, restaurant-size stockpot or divide between 2–4 large stockpots. Place on stove and heat over medium heat, stirring often. Heat until simmering. Simmer for 20–30 minutes before serving.

This is an easy chili recipe to make when serving a big crowd. The 6-lb. restaurant-size cans (also known as #10 cans) can be purchased at Costco, Sam's Club, or Cash and Carry. The meat and onions can be cooked ahead of time, and the canned ingredients can be added the day the chili is prepared. The chili can also be frozen in large resealable freezer bags and then thawed in the refrigerator overnight and reheated the day it is served.

CAKEY
CORNBREAD

3 15-oz. boxes yellow cake mix, unprepared
3 9-oz. boxes cornbread mix, unprepared
1 C. milk
12 eggs
1 C. butter (2 cubes), melted
3 C. water

(You will need three 9x13 pans or 2 muffin tins)

In an extra-large bowl, mix cake and cornbread mixes. Add remaining ingredients and stir well. The batter should be thick.

For Cakey Cornbread: Spray three 9x13 pans with non-stick cooking spray. Divide batter evenly between into prepared pans. Bake two pans side by side in the oven at 350 degrees for 20–25 minutes, or until a toothpick inserted in the center comes out clean. Remove from oven and cool while baking the third pan. Slice each cornbread cake into 15 square pieces. Serve warm or cold.

For Cornbread Muffins: Line two regular-size muffin tins (12 muffins each) with cupcake liners. Fill each liner approximately ⅔ full with cornbread batter. Bake at 350 degrees for 18–20 minutes or until light golden brown on top. Remove muffins from tins. Repeat to bake the remaining batter. This recipe should yield 45–48 cornbread muffins.

CHOCOLATE CHIP PUMPKIN
SHEET CAKE

Wet Ingredients:
1 15-oz. can pumpkin
2 C. sugar
½ C. vegetable oil
½ C. sour cream
4 eggs, beaten

Dry Ingredients:
2 C. flour
2 tsp. baking soda
2 tsp. cinnamon
¼ tsp. ginger
¼ tsp. nutmeg
½ tsp. salt

Other Ingredients:
1 12-oz. bag mini chocolate chips

Cream Cheese Frosting:
¼ C. butter, softened
1 8-oz. pkg. cream cheese, softened
1 tsp. vanilla
2 C. powdered sugar

This cake is the perfect recipe for holiday parties! Not only does it taste amazing, it feeds a crowd and looks pretty.

(You will need to make 2 cakes to serve 48)

Preheat oven to 350 degrees. Spray a cookie sheet (one with sides) with nonstick cooking spray. In a large bowl, beat wet ingredients. In a medium bowl, ombine dry ingredients. Add the dry mixture to the wet and mix thoroughly. Stir in chocolate chips. Pour the batter into the cookie sheet and bake 25–30 minutes or until a toothpick inserted in the center comes out clean. Let cool before frosting.

In a medium bowl, beat the frosting ingredients. Pour the frosting into a large plastic bag and cut a small hole in the corner. When the cake is completely cool, decorate it with the cream cheese frosting (see photo). Keep cake refrigerated until ready to serve.

Hawaiian Dinner and Dessert for 20-25

Hawaiian Kalua Pork with Cabbage is a dish often served at luaus. This version is made in the slow-cooker and tastes just like authentic shredded Kalua Pig. Don't worry if it is a tight squeeze in the slow-cooker; as long as you can get the lid on for a good seal, you are good to go. You can even cut the pork into two or three big pieces if you must to make it all fit. Or, depending on the size of your slow-cooker, you may have to cook the dish in two slow-cookers.

Our Cooking Rice for a Crowd (Easy Oven Method) recipe works great with the Kalua Pork because it can cook in the oven while the pork is cooking in the slow-cooker. For an even more authentic Hawaiian dinner, serve our L&L Barbecue Authentic Hawaiian Macaroni Salad from the July recipes as another side (it will need to be doubled to feed 24). Top it all off with our Orange Pineapple Sheet Cake. The cake is orange-flavored and moist, and the pineapple whipped topping is light and creamy—a perfect tropical combination!

HAWAIIAN
KALUA PORK
with Cabbage

SERVES
20-25

---

2 5- to 6-lb. pork roasts

4 T. Kosher salt

1 C. liquid smoke

3 C. water

2 heads cabbage, coarsely chopped

Rub pork generously with salt and pour on liquid smoke. Place in slow-cooker. Add water. Cover and cook on low 8–10 hours. An hour before serving, carefully lift pork out of the slow-cooker (do not drain out juices) and place cabbage in the bottom of the slow-cooker. Place pork on top of the cabbage, place lid back on, and cook for another hour. Shred pork and serve.

(EASY OVEN METHOD)
COOKING RICE
for a Crowd

1½ quarts long-grain white rice
2½ quarts water
1½ T. kosher salt

Preheat oven to 350 degrees. Spread uncooked rice evenly in a large roasting pan that has been lightly sprayed with nonstick cooking spray. Set aside. In a large stockpot, combine water and salt. Bring to a rolling boil. Carefully pour boiling water over rice and stir so rice is even along the bottom. Immediately cover with aluminum foil, making sure you have a tight seal around all the edges. Place roasting pan in oven and bake for 40–45 minutes, or until rice is tender. Fluff with a large wooden spoon and serve.

Note: If you want to wait to serve, keep rice warm in the oven at 150 degrees or keep warm in an electric warming pan. Add a little water if necessary to keep the rice from drying out.

SHARE YOUR FAVORITE CROWD RECIPES WITH YOUR FAMILY AT THE END OF THE SECTION.
Do you have a favorite lunch or dinner recipe you use when cooking for a large group?

ORANGE PINEAPPLE
CAKE

SERVES
20-24

1 15-oz. box lemon or yellow cake mix, unprepared
4 eggs
½ C. oil
1 8-oz. can mandarin oranges, undrained
1 3.9-oz. box instant vanilla pudding mix
1 15-oz. can crushed pineapple, undrained
1 16-oz. container whipped topping

Cake: Preheat oven to 325 degrees. Spray a 13 x 18 pan with nonstick cooking spray. In a large bowl, mix the first four ingredients. Pour batter into the pan and bake for 15 minutes. Let cake cool before frosting.

Frosting: In a mixer or with a blender, beat pudding mix, crushed pineapple, and whipped topping; spread generously over the cooled cake. Keep the frosted cake in the refrigerator until it is served.

FAVORITE FAMILY RECIPE

SERVES

{ RECIPE TITLE }

Ingredients:

Instructions:

FAVORITE FAMILY RECIPE

SERVES

_____

{ RECIPE TITLE }

Ingredients:

_____
_____
_____
_____
_____
_____
_____
_____
_____
_____
_____
_____
_____
_____
_____
_____
_____

Instructions:

_____
_____
_____
_____
_____
_____
_____
_____
_____
_____
_____
_____
_____
_____
_____
_____
_____
_____
_____
_____
_____

INDEX